HOCKEY FIGHT IN CANADA

HOCKEY FIGHT IN CANADA

The Big Media Faceoff over the NHL

David Shoalts

Douglas & McIntyre

Douglas and McIntyre (2013) Ltd.
P.O. Box 219, Madeira Park, BC, VON 2HO
www.douglas-mcintyre.com

Edited by Derek Fairbridge
Indexed by Brianna Cerkiewicz
Cover design by Anna Comfort O'Keeffe
Text design by Mary White
Printed in Canada

Douglas and McIntyre (2013) Ltd. acknowledges the support of the Canada Council for the Arts, which last year invested $153 million to bring the arts to Canadians throughout the country. We also gratefully acknowledge financial support from the Government of Canada and from the Province of British Columbia through the BC Arts Council and the Book Publishing Tax Credit.

Library and Archives Canada Cataloguing in Publication

Shoalts, David, author
     Hockey fight in Canada : the big media faceoff over the NHL / David Shoalts.

Includes index.
Issued in print and electronic formats.
ISBN 978-1-77162-204-2 (softcover).—ISBN 978-1-77162-205-9 (HTML)

     1. Television broadcasting of sports—Canada. 2. Hockey—Canada. 3. National Hockey League. 4. Hockey night in Canada (Television program). I. Title.

GV742.3.S56 2018   070.4'497969620971   C2018-902182-9
                                          C2018-902183-7

CONTENTS

PREFACE

Looking back on it, this story pretty much took me by surprise. The sports media beat at *The Globe and Mail* was a new one for me in the late fall of 2013 when change was in the air surrounding *Hockey Night in Canada*. Sports media people, including me, knew there was a good chance a CBC institution, and by extension a Canadian one, might be headed toward either BCE Inc., more familiarly known as Bell Canada, or Rogers Communications Inc.

In recent years, the price of sports broadcast rights exploded thanks to the fact they were practically the only remaining television properties that were best consumed live, not PVR'd for consumption at our leisure. Advertisers knew their commercials would get some sort of audience.

So we all knew the CBC, beleaguered by funding cuts from a hostile Stephen Harper government along with the usual decline in advertising revenue faced by all broadcasters, was unlikely to maintain control over *Hockey Night*. A lot of us figured the CBC would keep at least a piece of the show by becoming a junior partner to either Bell or Rogers. None of us saw what actually came to pass—Rogers bought total control of *Hockey Night in Canada* and the CBC meekly agreed to turn over its airwaves for free so it wouldn't have to replace Ron, Don and the rest of the program.

Something else I never saw coming was how this story resonated with Canadians. When the first articles written about the switch in NHL rights by my *Globe and Mail* colleagues and myself hit the *Globe*'s web site, they quickly rocketed to the top of the most-popular stories list. And, at times, stayed there for days.

As the first season under Rogers went on, the stories about how the CBC lost the rights over the summer and fall of 2013 continued to shoot to the top of those lists. The phenomenon continued over the next three years through the poor ratings for Rogers, thanks to the collective struggles of the Canadian teams and the ensuing fallout.

It was also not unusual for each one of those articles to draw dozens and even hundreds of comments from readers. Perhaps I shouldn't have been surprised, since the reason Rogers paid $5.2 billion (Canadian) for the NHL rights is it was convinced Canadians were so passionate about hockey the deal was worth it.

It turns out they are equally passionate about who brings them their hockey fix, especially on Saturday nights. So, speaking selfishly, I hope that passion continues for a long time yet. Fortunately, I think you will find there were enough twists and turns in the story of that sea change in *Hockey Night* and the related developments to reward your interest.

There are a lot of people to thank for helping bring this book together, but I would like to mention a few in particular. I must thank the publisher, Douglas and McIntyre, and my literary agent, Brian Wood, for their patience through this process. There were times, I am sure, my pleas for yet another deadline extension were aggravating in the extreme. However, I was also lucky enough that the delays meant some sources decided to impart information that made the book much better.

A number of people in the broadcast business were unselfish with their time and I thank them all. Among them were Keith Pelley, Scott Moore, Phil King, Stewart Johnston and Kirstine Stewart. Thank you, too, to John Collins, formerly the chief operating officer of the NHL and now the CEO of On Location Experiences. There were also several people in the same businesses who cannot be thanked by name due to the nature of the information they passed along. But without them much of this book would not have been possible.

I would also like to thank *The Globe and Mail*'s editor-in-chief David Walmsley and sports editor Shawna Richer for giving me permission to use the information for all those stories on the NHL rights in this book. Also, thank you, Shawna and assistant sports editor Jamie Ross for your patience as this project dragged on.

There is one person I am indebted to more than any other for allowing this to get finished. Or, more properly, pushing me to apply the seat of my pants to the seat of the chair in front of the computer. My wife, Yvonne Harris, was unfailingly patient in taking second place to this book for many months in the summer and fall of 2017, even when it included vacations. She was also diligent about kicking me out of bed at five o'clock every morning. Thank you.

Finally, I would like to thank my parents, Roy and Vivian Shoalts, for making me aware of the importance of the CBC at an early age by always having the radio tuned to the national broadcaster.

1

THE WARNING SHOT

Shortly before January 28, 2012, when the National Hockey League's board of governors would hold its traditional meeting during activities around the annual NHL All-Star Game, Brian Burke contacted Jeffrey Orridge, the head of sports for the CBC. It was not a routine call.

Burke, then the president and general manager of the Toronto Maple Leafs, could be blustery at the best of times. But this time he was all business. Burke warned Orridge, who had only been in the CBC job for about a year, the meeting in Ottawa was not going to be the usual all-star confab. Traditionally, as the NHL's major television rights-holder through *Hockey Night in Canada*, a show that has been part of almost every Canadian's Saturday night for more than 60 years, the CBC would send a few executives to the all-star festivities. They would spare some time from the cocktail parties to drop in on what was usually a housekeeping meeting for those running the NHL's 30 teams. Normally, the CBC team would make a short presentation to the NHL governors, a group that included not just the principal owners and chief executive officers of each team but usually a couple of other key executives like presidents and general managers if they carried the title of alternate governor. Sometimes the meetings could have 80 or more people in the room. The CBC representatives would talk about how well the broadcasts were going, outline the plans for the future and then, after some handshakes and backslapping, both the governors and the CBC executives would move on to the next event in the NHL's midseason break.

At the time, clouds were beginning to gather over the CBC's share of the national NHL broadcast rights in Canada. The contract with the NHL included not just the right to broadcast a package of the six Canadian teams' Saturday night games but the NHL All-Star Game, several other designated games on other nights and the Stanley Cup playoffs. This contract also included the digital rights, such as highlights on the CBC web site, which were in their infancy in 2012. The deal, which began in the 2007–08 season, paid the league $105 million per year from the CBC alone. It would be up at the end of the 2013–14 season. While the North American economy remained sluggish in the wake of the 2008 recession, rights fees for sports leagues were rising rapidly even though the television industry was in turmoil. The changing nature of how people watched television, particularly the prized demographic of millennials, those then aged 18 to 34, was sending shock waves through the industry. Terms like "cord-cutting" were now grimly popular as young people in particular cancelled their cable-television packages in favour of online streaming services like Netflix, Hulu and Amazon Prime, although Canadian viewers at the time were mostly limited to Netflix. Even older audiences were already recording television shows and zipping past the commercials when they watched the programs later.

Live sports, though, was resistant to this. There was no zipping and zapping with commercials when it came to watching your favourite team. It was still appointment television, as conventional scheduled broadcasts were now called. The sponsors' pitches still played out in full, even if you were off getting a beer. That is why the fees the networks paid to the four major North American professional sports leagues kept rising. Even the lesser leagues, like the Canadian Football League and Major League Soccer, were pulling in more money.

The richest professional league in the world, the National Football League, pulled in an eye-popping amount of money because it had more television viewers than anyone else. At the time of that NHL governors' meeting in Ottawa, the NFL made a total of $20.4 billion (US) per year from its broadcast deals with the CBS, NBC, Fox and ESPN networks. When those contracts expired in 2013, the NFL signed new agreements with the same networks that ran from 2014 until 2022. The NFL's take jumped to $39.6 billion, an astonishing increase of nearly double when the networks paying that money were dealing with shrinking viewership for all programs.

The NHL was doing well, too. League commissioner Gary Bettman brightened the NHL's American television picture in April 2011 when he agreed to a $2-billion (US), 10-year contract with NBC for the national US rights. This culminated a years-long struggle for a decent US television contract that began in 2005 for Bettman, who was appointed commissioner in February 1993 after he sold the NHL owners on his plan to get such a TV deal by expanding the league into cities that did not have much hockey history but were large television markets, like Phoenix and Miami/Fort Lauderdale.

Despite his sometimes stiff and uncomfortable public appearances (breezy banter was not his strong suit in his early years as commissioner), Bettman was a formidable negotiator, canny businessman and tough leader behind closed doors. The NBC deal was a spectacular success, considering that in the summer of 2005 the giant US cable sports network ESPN essentially tossed the NHL aside when it was coming out of the season-long 2004–05 lockout.

Network executives haughtily offered Bettman $30 million (US) per year in a new contract, down sharply from the $70 million in the previous deal. Bettman does not respond well to such insults, which the ESPN people may have known full well, and told the network where to put its offer.

Bettman managed to get another deal in short order that started in the 2005–06 season with the cable network then known as the Outdoor Life Network for $65 million (US). But OLN was seen in far fewer homes than ESPN. By 2011, with around $190 million coming in annually for the Canadian national rights from CBC and the two sports cable networks owned by Bell Canada through its subsidiary company Bell Media, TSN and the French-language Réseau des sports (RDS), the NBC contract gave the league a total of $390 million per year in mixed currency by 2013. Not NFL money for sure, but a healthy sum considering the NHL was still considered by many US broadcast executives to be a regional attraction in the United States.

Times were good at the lesser end of the scale, too. Without a nice payout from TSN for exclusive television rights, the CFL's survival would have been in question. This provided the sports network with a large block of programming that was still relatively cheap compared to the cost of producing original content. By 2013, TSN paid $17 million to the CFL in the last year of its broadcast contract, which went a long way to covering the $4.4-million payroll limit of each team. In the same year, TSN struck a new five-year deal beginning in 2014 that pays the CFL an average of nearly $38 million per year. On a percentage basis, that easily beat the raise scored by the NFL.

Then again, Rogers Media president Keith Pelley and Sportsnet president Scott Moore might have had a hand in the CFL's windfall in addition to the trend to higher payouts. Along with making a run at the NHL in 2013, Pelley and Moore also took a look at getting a piece of the CFL action. There was talk of a Thursday night CFL broadcast on Sportsnet, but that ended when TSN got wind of it and quickly re-upped with the CFL. However, Pelley's motivation was not necessarily to bring the CFL to Sportsnet one night a week since the network schedule was already full with Toronto Blue Jays games. But the idea of forcing TSN to pay more in a new CFL contract was appealing, especially since it might make less money available for an NHL bid in a cost-conscious public company.

Being aggressive was no longer something the CBC could contemplate. It was strictly on the defensive thanks to the same problems the private broadcasters were dealing with plus a far more troublesome issue. As Canada's public broadcaster, the CBC receives the bulk of its funding from the federal government. In 2012, the annual federal subsidy to the CBC was $1.1 billion. The network's total advertising revenue was estimated to be around $450 million, with about $175 million of that coming from *Hockey Night in Canada*. But Prime Minister Stephen Harper and his Conservative Party did not spare the network from their cuts to the federal budget as the Canadian economy remained in the doldrums. In their 2012 budget, the Conservatives announced a 10-per-cent cut for the CBC over the next three years, a total of $115 million. While this was not the worst budget cut in the CBC's history—ones in the mid-1990s by the Liberal government of Jean Chrétien were deeper—the network was in a better position back then to withstand the pain because advertising revenue was still solid.

But there were more problems than money for the CBC when it came to the NHL, which is why Burke reached out to Orridge. Burke knew this meeting was going to be different than the usual glad-handing. He warned the head of CBC Sports that there was much unhappiness toward the network on the part of the then six Canadian NHL teams. Orridge was going to hear about it at the meeting.

The CBC boss may not have been overly worried about Burke's warning at first. The New York City native and Harvard law graduate had a background in sports marketing and had the easy manner of a marketing executive. Those who knew him said he was skilled at turning on the charm in social situations and quickly winning over new business acquaintances.

However, the Canadian teams' anger went beyond the usual complaints that the network favoured the Toronto Maple Leafs over the other five teams. Now there was great unhappiness with the broadcasts themselves and with broadcasters Don Cherry and Ron MacLean in particular.

For years, from his seat on the most popular segment of any hockey show in Canada (some call it a bully pulpit), Cherry made no secret of his love for the Maple Leafs. He also issued strong opinions on any number of topics, notably his support for fighting, including his thoughts on politics and the military, which had long exasperated his bosses at the CBC. From the day he joined *Hockey Night* full-time in 1981, Cherry became a beloved character just about everywhere in Canada, save for Québec thanks to his views on some francophone players. In 2004, the CBC aired a show called *The Greatest Canadian,* which surveyed viewers for a list of the country's greatest citizens. Cherry clocked in at No. 7, even ahead of Wayne Gretzky.

Cherry, who turned 84 in February 2018, came to *Hockey Night in Canada* after a six-year career as an NHL head coach with the Boston Bruins and the Colorado Rockies. He was easily the most flamboyant head coach in the NHL, a stubborn but endearing fellow who played up his image as the common man despite his love for three-piece suits. Cherry even bore a certain resemblance to his beloved bull terrier, Blue, whom he celebrated constantly on the air as the embodiment of determination and courage. The ex-coach's conservative views translated easily to television, where his love of fighting and dislike of European players went over well with most viewers.

Since Cherry was an unabashed Leafs fan, he did not make an ideal impartial analyst on the Saturday night broadcasts. But in what proved to be a stroke of genius, *Hockey Night* executive producer Ralph Mellanby created a show just for Cherry, where he could express his opinion (or rant) on whatever topic struck his fancy. During the first-period intermission, *Coach's Corner* quickly became must-see viewing and as Cherry's popularity exploded so did the garishness of his sports jackets, which quickly became the biggest part of his image.

While Cherry's views often clashed with those running the NHL, particularly after Gary Bettman became commissioner, he was tolerated and even liked by many in management. His immense popularity protected Cherry, as those at the top of the league did not care to alienate a large chunk of the fan-base. But the feelings about MacLean on the part of the NHL's team owners and executives appeared to be deeper and stronger.

As the host of *Hockey Night in Canada* as well as Cherry's sidekick on the *Coach's Corner* segment, MacLean was the face of the show, which by 2012 was a well-established national institution. What angered the Canadian NHL governors most of all was MacLean's unapologetic support for the players on just about every issue. This led to many an uncomfortable on-air confrontation with commissioner Bettman.

While MacLean could come across as homespun, usually when he was making one of his beloved puns, and would often defer to the fiery Cherry, that manner could vanish during interviews. MacLean did not hesitate to challenge the commissioner in any discussion about issues between the players and management. The live interviews often grew heated, especially when negotiations for a new collective agreement were at hand, which often meant a delayed or cancelled season thanks to an owners' lockout.

This reached a climax during the Stanley Cup Final on June 2, 2010, when Bettman was interviewed by MacLean during the second-period intermission of Game 3 between the Chicago Blackhawks and the Philadelphia Flyers. The interview began amiably enough, with MacLean singing "Happy Birthday" to Bettman to mark his 58th birthday. But it did not take long for the tension to rise when MacLean began asking Bettman about a few of the league's financial headaches like the perpetually struggling Phoenix Coyotes. Bettman grew testy and asked MacLean why he was pursuing that line of questioning because he didn't think most viewers were interested. MacLean said it was because the players were interested. Bettman suggested a better topic would be the players' performances in the playoffs. Then MacLean brought up the issue of a second NHL team for Southern Ontario, saying this was another topic of interest to the NHL players. Bettman's ire increased.

"Wait, who are you getting your information from as to what the players are thinking?" Bettman said. "You're making this up."

Shortly after the interview ended, Bettman made it known to the CBC brass he would never appear on *Hockey Night in Canada* again. And he never did for the last four years the CBC owned the show. MacLean said his clashes with Bettman were always driven by his journalistic instincts. He felt the players needed a voice on the biggest hockey show in Canada and that the NHL itself was healthier when the players' union was strong. He also said it was common for his bosses at the CBC to tell him to make nice with Bettman and the NHL, an interesting approach given the public network's concern with remaining an independent voice despite its government funding.

"That pressure was always there to acquiesce, to toe the company line and in some cases that might have been the league line," MacLean said. "But I felt strongly about the importance of a healthy NHL Players' Association. That was a difficult thing for both the CBC and the league to accept, always was. Nobody [at the CBC] was ever happy when I was treating a partner [with skepticism], a partner that thought they were more important than the NHLPA."

The Canadian NHL owners and their executives saw this as MacLean badgering Bettman unnecessarily. They also felt the host of the most important hockey broadcast in Canada should not show favouritism for one side over another. One NHL governor, who declined to be identified because Bettman does not like NHL business aired in public, said MacLean's support for the players and their union "drove teams crazy." However, if MacLean were consistently pro-management it is a good bet the NHL owners and managers would be far more sanguine about that sort of favouritism.

John Collins, then the NHL's chief operating officer and head of marketing, also thought the CBC's relationship with the league needed to improve. Collins, who is said to have one of the best marketing minds in sports by many of his colleagues, joined the NHL in 2006 after a long career in the NFL, where he went from a job with NFL Films to become president of the Cleveland Browns and then moved to the league's head office. He became head of the hugely successful league's marketing, promotion, advertising and sponsorship programs. During his NFL days, Collins was accustomed to a more cordial attitude toward the league from its broadcast partners. The US networks carrying NFL games were notorious for their aversion to airing controversial issues on their football broadcasts. Issues like the concussion lawsuit brought against the league by former players, the use of performance-enhancing drugs and the national anthem protests are covered only reluctantly by the NFL's network partners.

While there were a number of CBC executives over the years who tried to rein in Cherry and MacLean, the network's overall treatment of the NHL was nothing like what the NFL enjoyed. MacLean and Cherry weren't the only critics, as league issues were regularly debated on the intermission panels like *Satellite*

Hotstove. Collins said the list of complaints by the Canadian teams was growing.

"For anybody other than Toronto there were grievances about the schedule and the kind of exposure their teams weren't getting," Collins said. "There were issues about the editorial coverage, in particular the shots that were taken at the general managers themselves and overall at the league."

League executives like Bettman and Collins also felt *Hockey Night* did not put enough emphasis on the players themselves and their stories. It was all Ron and Don and the panel discussions rather than more features on the men who played the game. *Hockey Night* producers and broadcasters would argue there was lots of attention to the players in features and interviews that ran on the pre-game show and on Scott Oake's *After Hours* show that came on after the second game of the Saturday night doubleheader.

Burke didn't have much to say about the Leafs' scheduling on *Hockey Night.* His team was regularly shown in the first game of the Saturday doubleheader, always the highest-rated game of the week, because it represented the largest television market in Canada. Ever since games were shown on television in Canada starting in 1952, it was the Maple Leafs who drove the ratings. But Burke was unhappy in the extreme with Cherry and MacLean over what he saw as unfair criticism of him, the Toronto Maple Leafs and their head coach, Ron Wilson.

The irony was that Burke's approach to the game was almost the same as Cherry's. A large, tempestuous man who favoured an unbuttoned appearance with his tie perpetually draped around his neck rather than tied under his collar, Burke liked big, tough physical players who could not only skate with their opponents but pound them into the boards as well. When Burke was GM of the Anaheim Ducks, they won the 2007 Stanley Cup with physically imposing players like Chris Pronger and Ryan Getzlaf who also had lots of hockey skills. Any mention of the gruff, volatile Burke in a story or on social or regular media often included the word "truculence," Burke's favourite descriptor of his ideal team.

The problem was, even though Cherry liked the same style of hockey as Burke and was an unabashed Leafs fan to boot, the Leafs GM was an American. So was Burke's good friend Ron Wilson, the head coach, although they both hold dual US-Canadian citizenship. The way Cherry saw it, Burke and Wilson were using too many American players in their rebuild of the Maple Leafs at the expense of Canadians. To the great Canadian patriot Cherry, this was unthinkable. "That's the way I am and I'm not making any excuses for it. I like Ontario guys. Every team has Ontario guys. I still say it's ridiculous that we don't have any up here," Cherry said on Toronto radio station Sportsnet The Fan 590 one Monday morning after the feud heated up again the previous Saturday on *Coach's Corner.*

Rebuilding the perennially mediocre Leafs was the NHL's version of a Sisyphean task and Burke was left a particularly messy list of bad player contracts when he took over in November 2008. The going was slow, which also left lots of room for Cherry and MacLean to criticize the team. The criticism often veered into other areas, which angered Burke even more. At every Leafs home game, a member of the Canadian military is honoured during a timeout and shown on the giant scoreboard video screen, which draws a long round of applause from the Air Canada Centre crowd. One night Cherry accused Wilson of not showing his respect for the featured Canadian soldier by failing to applaud. Burke was incensed more than usual by this one, since he prides himself as a strong supporter of the men and women in the military, yet another irony in his war with Cherry. Burke told people that Wilson did indeed applaud the soldier but turned his attention to instructing his players before the timeout was over. The camera did not pan to Wilson until he was finished clapping, according to Burke, so Cherry was mistaken.

Add all of the slights together and Burke was primed and pumped by the time the NHL governors' meeting began in an Ottawa hotel conference room on the Saturday morning of the 2012 NHL all-star weekend. Leading the CBC's delegation were Jeffrey Orridge, the head of the sports department, and executive vice-president Kirstine Stewart, the head of CBC English services. The CBC came up early on the agenda and the governors were given a presentation by the CBC executives about the many fine things the network was doing for the league. Then the governors had the floor. Burke spoke first. He made a heated denunciation of Cherry, MacLean and the network. Burke used words like "unprofessional," "anti-American," "intolerable" and so on. It was delivered at the usual high volume that comes when Burke is wound up.

"Brian went at them," Collins said. "Brian was so hot and certainly poured gasoline on the fire there as Brian can do."

What made this notable, however, is that other governors from Canadian teams took the floor after Burke and voiced similar complaints as well as the usual bellyaching about the Leafs getting too much love from the CBC. A Vancouver Canucks governor followed Burke—memories of the closed-door meeting are now vague but most say it was GM Mike Gillis rather than team owner Francesco Aquilini—and he supported everything Burke said. The significance of this is that there was no love lost between the Canucks and Burke, who was fired as Vancouver's GM in 2004 shortly before Aquilini bought a share of the team. Ottawa Senators owner Eugene Melnyk also took the floor, although he told *The Globe and Mail* he confined his blast of the CBC to how little his team was shown on the network compared to the Leafs.

"It got a little warm in there," Edmonton Oilers president Pat LaForge told *The Globe and Mail*. "If NHL realignment was a 3 on the Richter emotional scale, this was a 5." But LaForge added it was not unusual for the NHL governors' meetings to get heated.

Perhaps, but it was certainly unusual for the governors to go off on a league partner. With negotiations for a new television contract coming up within six months, the governors' unhappiness should have been an early warning for the CBC executives that holding on to the lion's share of the NHL's national broadcast rights was not going to be easy. There were already lots of rumours in the broadcast and hockey communities as well as in the media that Bell Canada and Rogers Communications Inc., the Sportsnet owner, were going to put their overwhelming financial might behind bids for the prize for their sports networks. But Collins did not get the sense that Orridge and Stewart saw it the same way.

"There just seemed to be a huge disconnect in the room," Collins said. "The CBC guys came in with the feeling they were doing a great job, they were there very benignly to talk about the good work they'd been doing and the overall vision in terms of where CBC was going.

"I don't think they ever considered that just kind of laying there in ambush were a bunch of the Canadian clubs in particular, who just had felt like there was a whole list of grievances. There was simmering anger in the room about how could you walk in as a partner and ignore that. I think that was the biggest part of it."

Stewart thought the governors seemed more concerned with their own teams rather than holding any deep-seated resentment about how the CBC covered the league as a whole. She also thought the complaints by Burke and others about Cherry and MacLean were just venting, something that could be worked out.

"From my perspective and what I remember, there were certainly complaints from different owners about how much their team was covered," Stewart said. "But that was certainly what you would expect from any roundtable where you've got anybody from Ottawa to every team around the table and they're wondering how come you're focusing on the Leafs and Habs. That was the temper of the conversation, you seem to favour these two but what about the rest of us? They all wanted their fair shake at what they considered prime time on CBC."

In Stewart's view, the CBC was always interested in a good working relationship with the NHL. When the NHL did well, so did the CBC in the form of good television ratings. Indeed, both she and Orridge had good working relationships with Bettman and Collins and there was mutual respect between them. But at the same time, Stewart felt, the NHL had no business trying to tell the network how it should cover the league, its teams, its players and its issues.

"As the rights-holder and the broadcaster, you look at it as, was it fair?" she said. "Ultimately the job of *Hockey Night* was to cover hockey and they weren't going to be dictated to [by the NHL], as long as it was fair. No, any of the complaints [the NHL] had were the same issues they'd have with any broadcaster. If you cover any sport beyond the PR, you are going to encounter that kind of friction.

"I never got the impression that if Bell or Rogers were to become the next owners, the league would have any more say over how the show went. I think they would be incredibly naïve to think they'd have more say in how that happened."

As it would turn out, the NHL was after a lot more say in how the next rights-holder would broadcast its games. But that was months away. Collins came away from the meeting with the belief Stewart and Orridge did not see the long-term significance of the attitude of the Canadian governors. But he understood why certain signals, like the support of the Canucks for something Brian Burke said, were missed. As the head of CBC's English services, Stewart did not have a lot of direct contact with NHL people and her mandate certainly did not require her to keep a finger on the league's pulse. That was Orridge's responsibility. But he was only one year into his job as the boss of CBC Sports and although he knew Bettman from his days working for USA Basketball when Bettman was an NBA executive, the NHL was still new to him. Orridge must have felt blindsided by the vitriol because he complained to Burke afterward that his warning about the governors was not strong enough.

"It wasn't traditional," Collins said of the CBC delegation, which did not include Trevor Pilling, the executive producer of *Hockey Night* at the time. "It was the CBC leadership for sure but it wasn't the hockey guys. The hockey guys might have been more aware and might have debated the [tone of the CBC's NHL broadcasts]."

While the meeting ended with both sides promising further discussions, it appears the only meetings to follow were between Burke and Orridge over Burke's unhappiness with Cherry and MacLean. And that is where most of the media's interest lay, especially since the war between Cherry and the Leafs boss escalated quickly after the Ottawa session, fuelled in part by media reports that Burke filed an official complaint about Cherry with the CBC.

Given the outsized and bellicose personalities involved, the Burke-Cherry feud moved to the front of the sports sections in the Toronto newspapers in February and March 2012. Since the Maple Leafs under Ron Wilson were in the process of becoming "an 18-wheeler going right off a cliff," in Burke's famous phrase, Cherry had lots of ammunition. The climax came on *Coach's Corner* on March 2, the night after the Leafs' long slide out of playoff contention was punctuated by Burke firing Wilson.

In what turned out to be a warm-up to the Cherry-Burke main event, MacLean conducted a live interview with Burke about Wilson's firing. Burke has told colleagues that shortly before he went on the air, MacLean told him he only planned to ask him a few innocuous questions about Wilson's replacement, Randy Carlyle, who was Burke's head coach with the Ducks when they won the 2007 Stanley Cup. Instead, MacLean opened the interview by asking if firing Wilson was not a form of making excuses for the poor performances of the Leafs players. Then the questioning veered into why the Maple Leafs did not have more Ontario-born players in their system and on the team, Cherry's pet peeve. While MacLean had every right to ask any question he wanted, and Burke has never been known to demand a list of questions before interviews, the Leafs boss felt he was ambushed. When the interview ended, Burke vowed off-camera, just as Gary Bettman had almost two years earlier, never to appear on *Hockey Night* again.

After the first period, Cherry opened his show with his guns blazing: "Here's what kills me—Burke goes to my bosses and says I'm a bad guy because I said something 'vicious', I think the words were, about his coach ... Two weeks later he fires him. Figure that one out, folks."

Cherry came back to Burke a few minutes later and accused him of trying to get him fired. "You want to get me off? You want to take me on?" Cherry said. "Oh Brian Burke, I'm shaking in my boots. Do your best."

Cherry was correct in his belief that his job with the CBC was safe from outside pressure. But both Burke and Orridge maintained since the governors' meeting in Ottawa that the Leafs boss never demanded Cherry be fired. Burke always said he just wanted Cherry forced to be fair in his criticism of Burke, Wilson and the Leafs.

From there, Cherry picked up on his favourite chestnut about the Leafs and Ontario-born players. At the time, there were no such players on the Leafs' roster. Cherry went through a list of NHL teams and how many Ontario players each one had and how awful it was that the team in the biggest city in Ontario had none.

Since this was Don Cherry and *Coach's Corner*, the most-watched hockey commentary show in Canada, many other media outlets fanned the flames. The contretemps resulted in lots of headlines and hot air on radio and television. Burke fired back, of course, with a typical salvo coming a few days later when he appeared on Toronto radio station NewsTalk 1010's morning show. Burke told host John Moore he was in charge of three NHL entry drafts for the Leafs from 2009 through 2011. "In those three drafts that I've been here, we lead the league with eight Ontario-born players drafted," Burke said. "So the notion that we don't like Ontario kids, that's garbage."

Burke was correct, of course, and with better work from his scouts he might have been able to squelch Cherry's complaints. But the Ontario kids were not good enough as a group either then, when none of them could make the Leafs' roster, or later. Of those eight Ontario-born players, only two made the Leafs for any appreciable time and only one, centre Nazem Kadri who was picked in the first round in 2009, became an important player. Both Kadri and forward Josh Leivo were still with the Leafs by the start of the 2017–18 season, although Leivo was a fringe player with just 41 regular-season games played over four seasons. The other six players managed a combined total of 104 NHL games played. Most of those games were compiled by forward Greg McKegg, who played 65 games with three different NHL teams by the end of the 2016–17 season. Only four were for the Maple Leafs.

Burke and his scouts added three more Ontarians in the June 2012 draft, the last one he handled for the team before getting fired in January 2013, although the controversy had run its course by then. But their fourth-round pick, forward Connor Brown, a hometown boy from Toronto, joined Kadri as a key member of the resurgent Leafs.

The Cherry-Burke feud distracted almost all of the media that covered league and broadcasting issues in the weeks and months following the NHL governors' meeting in Ottawa. Only one writer, *The Globe and Mail*'s freelance media columnist Bruce Dowbiggin, also noted the unhappiness of the Canadian teams and the league went far beyond MacLean and Cherry. Dowbiggin drew a line connecting the discontent shown at the Ottawa meeting and the CBC's prospects of signing a new broadcast deal with the NHL. The league felt *Hockey Night* was too wrapped up in the personalities of its broadcasters, with MacLean and Cherry leading the way in airtime, and not concerned enough with the players and the teams.

Even though the Canadian NHL owners were not happy with the CBC and the rumours about Bell's and Rogers' plans to use their wealth to snatch away *Hockey Night in Canada* were growing, few people seriously thought there would be a day when the CBC actually lost the show. There was just too much history there.

While radio broadcasts of Toronto Maple Leafs games started in 1923, the roots of *Hockey Night in Canada* began in 1929 when team owner Conn Smythe sold the radio rights of his games to advertising man Jack MacLaren beginning in 1931 when Maple Leaf Gardens was built. The price was $500 and the deal was concluded over nine holes of golf. By this time, Foster Hewitt was well established as the play-by-play man. Once MacLaren took over in 1931 the games went national and the show was called the *General Motors Hockey Broadcast* after the major sponsor. In 1936 the games moved to the newly formed CBC's radio network and the show became *Hockey Night in Canada*, a title coined by Hewitt. The broadcasts did not start until 9 p.m., when the second period was under way, because Smythe thought ticket sales would be hurt if Hewitt could be heard at the opening faceoff. The Leafs' games were broadcast in Ontario and to the west, while the CBC's French network carried the Montreal Canadiens in Québec.

This started the Canadian cultural tableau of entire families gathered around the radio to hear their favourite team. This warm and fuzzy image really gained steam in the 1950s when the games moved to CBC television. The first televised game in Canada was on October 11, 1952, when Rene Lecavalier called the match between the Canadiens and the Detroit Red Wings in French. English Canada joined the party almost a month later, on November 1, 1952, when Hewitt called the Leafs–Boston Bruins game.

The next major technological advance came in the 1966–67 season when the games were shown in colour. However, it was a couple more years before viewers could see the games in full. The power of the NHL owners was such that *Hockey Night in Canada* was not able to persuade them to allow the broadcasts to start with the opening faceoff at 8 p.m. until the 1968–69 season.

An oddity about the show is the CBC never actually owned it until 1994. The *Hockey Night* brand was actually owned by MacLaren Advertising for almost 60 years, after that first deal with Smythe in 1929, even though the games were produced in partnership with the CBC. In 1986, Molstar Communications, a subsidiary of Molson Brewery, took over the show from MacLaren and in 1994 the CBC bought it from Molstar.

The discontent registered at the NHL governors' meeting in Ottawa was not necessarily going to be a deal-breaker for the CBC. One of Bettman's strengths as a negotiator is that even though he has a fine sense of what sort of respect should be shown to both him and the league, he never lets it get in the way of the best possible deal for the NHL.

"Gary certainly never would have raised that as an issue, the fact Ron [MacLean] would go after him. Gary never would have personalized that issue," Collins said. "There were certainly people who took up the mantle for him and just could never imagine that happening in another league with another marquee network partner in the middle of your championship moment taking shots, kind of looking for a way to create some controversy. That was in the room [in Ottawa]."

But by the end of the all-star weekend, Collins did not think the depth of the NHL's dissatisfaction and its implications for the broadcast rights were going to be understood by those at the top of the CBC. "Look, it clearly was a warning shot and it wasn't viewed that way [by the CBC]," Collins said of the Ottawa meeting. The unhappiness "went deeper" than simple anger from team executives over critical remarks by Cherry or MacLean. "There were a lot of questions about the nature of the relationship," Collins added.

2

THE GATHERING STORM

When the negotiating period for the next NHL Canadian national broadcast rights contract hove into view in the spring of 2013, there was one assurance for the eventual winner. It would play out the new deal without the threat of a labour disruption. Or at least most of it, anyway.

After wiping out 510 games of the 2012–13 season by locking out the players, NHL commissioner Gary Bettman settled on a new collective agreement on January 6, 2013 with Donald Fehr, executive director of the NHL Players' Association. The major issue for the owners was to reduce the players' share of the NHL's hockey-related revenue, which was 57 per cent in the previous contract. The players agreed to a 50-50 split with the owners in the new deal. It would run for 10 years, with both the players and the owners having the right to opt out of it after eight years. That meant whoever landed the next Canadian national NHL rights contract, which would begin in the 2014–15 season, was guaranteed six full seasons of NHL hockey and eight if both sides remained happy with the deal. Not bad by NHL standards, considering this was the third lockout since Bettman became commissioner in 1993.

Also, in 2013 most of the big broadcast deals being signed were for around seven (Major League Baseball) or eight (NFL) years. One exception was the 10-year contract the NHL had with NBC, which in retrospect should have been an indication of where things were headed in hockey. Still, the prospect of at least six uninterrupted seasons offered some reassurance for the media companies because a lockout is an expensive business for all concerned. For example, the CBC reported a loss of $43 million in revenue in its 2012–13 financial statement. Most of this was attributed to the NHL lockout, which reduced the 82-game season by 40 per cent to 48 games.

The negotiations for the new NHL deal were set to open in July 2013. As the existing majority rights-holder, the CBC had an exclusive negotiating period with the NHL until the end of August. After that, the bidding was open, which was when Bell Media and Rogers Media, the only other serious bidders, could join the party.

By this point, both the hockey and broadcasting worlds had seen months of upheaval. While the NHL was dealing with its labour problems in late 2012, the changes in how and when people watched television were starting to hit home for the broadcast and cable companies. Since Rogers and BCE were both broadcast and cable companies in addition to being Internet and telephone providers, they took a full dose of the changes. The fact that both conglomerates were made up of all of the above industries meant they continued to roll in the profits, but it did mean that some divisions, cable in particular, were taking heavy hits. And in a publicly traded company, every division is expected to pull its weight and the leaders of those divisions are only as good as their latest quarter. If your earnings slip in a quarter, particularly EBITDA—earnings before interest, taxes, depreciation and amortization, which is a benchmark of a company's health—then hard looks come from the chairman and the board of directors. A few too many bad quarters and it's time to polish the resumé. But compared to what the CBC faced, the Bell and Rogers problems were merely some discomfort. The national broadcaster did not have Internet, telephone and mobile sales to offset its losses and faced a lot of difficult decisions in cutting its budgets due to shrinking advertising revenues and government subsidies.

Rogers Communications president and chief executive officer Nadir Mohamed had no hand in the company's cable woes (25,000 customers cancelled their cable packages in the final quarter of 2012), as he rose to stardom by presiding over the hugely successful wireless division. When he was appointed CEO in 2009, Mohamed was the clear choice of the late Ted Rogers, the daring company founder who made enormous risky bets with his business over the years but won most of them. Mohamed was as carefully bland as his mentor Rogers was colourful and given to bold statements and actions. By the time of his death of congestive heart failure in December 2008 at the age of 75, Ted Rogers built his eponymous company from a single Toronto radio station (CHFI) in the early 1960s into an $18-billion conglomerate with a range of services from digital TV to Internet to wireless to cable to media and sports properties like the Toronto Blue Jays and their retractable-dome stadium, rechristened the Rogers Centre.

Two of Rogers' four children, Edward and Melinda, worked at Rogers Communications at the time of his death. Edward was named CEO of Rogers Cable in 2003, while Melinda founded and ran a venture capital arm of the company, called Rogers Venture Partners, based in San Francisco.

According to a profile of the Rogers family published by *Toronto Life* magazine in October 2014, Edward Rogers III wanted to succeed his father as CEO of the family company. While Ted hoped one of his children would eventually succeed him, he did not think Edward was ready by the close of the first decade of the

2000s. Ted thought Mohamed, whom he hired away from upstart wireless competitor Telus in 2000 to run Rogers' wireless division, was a better choice. Mohamed's experience in running the smaller and more nimble Telus operation, particularly when it came to the fast-growing wireless field, was considered more suited to guiding Rogers.

In the *Toronto Life* story and other media reports, Ted Rogers and Mohamed were described as the perfect match. Even though he came from an aggressive company like Telus, which was making serious gains on Rogers and BCE in the fight for the mobile telephone business, Mohamed was by nature a conservative, cautious businessman. He proved to be a counterbalance to a mercurial dealmaker like Ted.

The wireless division saw its profits explode under Mohamed, who moved Rogers away from pre-paid wireless contracts to post-paid contracts. A post-paid contract means the wireless customer is billed for their use at the end of the month and any minutes or data above a specified amount is charged at a higher rate. This brought in steadily rising profits for the company. Mohamed and Ted also hit the jackpot in 2004 when they bought Microcell, which at the time was the only Canadian provider of GSM network technology aside from Rogers. In 2008, this gave Rogers the monopoly on selling the iPhone, which used GSM, when Apple launched it in Canada.

While Mohamed was enjoying a long run of success, Edward was stuck with Rogers' cable division, which was beginning to feel the effects of customers moving away from conventional television. The cord-cutting, as it came to be known, gained steam a few years later in 2010 when Netflix became the first major streaming service in Canada. These services only required an internet connection. While the wireless division saw its revenues grow by 155 per cent from 2004 to 2010, with the cable division showing decent but not spectacular profits, Edward's resentment grew, according to *Toronto Life*, creating not just a divide between the cable and wireless divisions but between him and Mohamed. This became worse when Ted promoted Mohamed to Rogers' chief operating officer, a signal for his preference for the next CEO.

Ted Rogers was plagued all his life by poor health, which made him acutely aware of the necessity of a succession plan. So he put together a family trust, which owned 91 per cent of the Rogers Class A voting shares. The trust was run by Ted, his wife, Loretta, their children and a group of trusted friends and advisors. Like most big companies, Rogers had dual-class shares, sort of the investors' way of having their cake and eating it, too. Class A shares had the voting rights along with a slice of the company, while Class B shares carried only a piece of the company. Thus owning the Class A shares kept the family in control of the company, while the trading of the Class B shares brought in the wealth. Ted Rogers' successors needed to remember this to ensure their longevity.

Officially, Ted Rogers decreed the company's board of directors would choose his successor after he died. Unofficially, he told senior executives and major investors in the company he preferred Mohamed as the next CEO. Edward, according to *Toronto Life*, could serve under Mohamed until it was determined he was ready for the captain's seat. But Edward made things awkward after Ted died by telling the board he wanted to be CEO.

Just how awkward the situation was can be seen in the length of time it took to appoint the new CEO. The board of directors formed a hiring committee but it took two months before Mohamed was confirmed, in line with Ted's wishes, as the new president and CEO of Rogers Communications. Mohamed reorganized the company, amalgamating the cable and wireless divisions, and shuffled Edward and Melinda into new jobs. Edward was now executive vice-president of emerging business and corporate development while Melinda became senior vice-president of strategy.

But as *Toronto Life* reported, the new look did little to endear Mohamed to Edward and Melinda, even though his more cautious approach than his predecessor, lowering the company's famous high debt ratio for one thing, did wonders for Rogers' value. Edward never attended any of Mohamed's compulsory quarterly meetings, where each division head would report its progress. Melinda made the effort to attend a few times but usually sent an underling.

Mohamed's reluctance to continue Ted Rogers' practice of buying up smaller competitors and other businesses to spur the company's growth was something else that made the Rogers family reluctant to warm up to him. The only major deal Mohamed consummated during his five years at the helm was the joint purchase with BCE of 75 per cent of Maple Leaf Sports and Entertainment (MLSE), the company that owned the Maple Leafs, the NBA's Toronto Raptors, Toronto FC of Major League Soccer and the Air Canada Centre. Rogers and BCE paid a total of $1.32 billion for the majority share of MLSE. Part of the deal saw construction tycoon Larry Tanenbaum, the chairman of MLSE, boost his stake from 20 to 25 per cent as the third owner. In exchange for dropping his right of first refusal when the Ontario Teachers' Pension Plan (OTPP) put its majority stake in MLSE up for sale in 2011, Tanenbaum was thought to have negotiated himself into the chairman's post for as long as he wanted plus a 5-per-cent bump in his shares.

The sale for MLSE went on for much of 2011 with Rogers and BCE eventually emerging as the reluctant main bidders. Bell Canada's George Cope, an intimidating fellow whose large frame suited his reputation as a hard-driving CEO, developed his chops at Telus, like Mohamed. Also like Mohamed, Cope was unwilling to throw unlimited money at the MLSE deal. So the fight for MLSE went dormant for long periods, as the OTPP, one of the wealthiest pension plans in the world, wanted to maximize its profits and was in no hurry to sell.

In the end, when it looked like Mohamed had a shot at grabbing the majority stake of MLSE for Rogers, Cope was convinced by other executives at Bell to jump in to prevent their rivals from grabbing the prize. If either company had been able to land MLSE by itself, it would have controlled most of the top sports programming in Toronto—the Maple Leafs, Raptors and Toronto FC.

Indeed, if Mohamed had been more aggressive, he could have had most of those teams' games for Rogers' Sportsnet plus the Blue Jays, which were wholly owned by Rogers. This would have left Bell Media's TSN in a much weakened state when its share of the NHL national rights expired at the end of the 2013–14 season. The TSN deal gave the network the right to broadcast 70 NHL games nationally on nights other than Saturday when the CBC held sway. TSN also broadcast the NHL draft and had a share with the CBC of the first two rounds of the playoffs, with the CBC having sole rights to the last two rounds. The other interesting what-if was that if either Rogers or Bell grabbed MLSE for itself, it would have been in position to tell Gary Bettman he could not hold it for ransom on the next deal for the NHL rights because that company would already control 52 Leafs regional games along with the Raptors and TFC.

However, both Cope and Mohamed were nervous about buying MLSE outright, given the $1.32-billion price tag. And neither man had any interest in getting into a bidding war with the other. Cope was fresh from spending $3.2 billion on reacquiring the broadcast arm of CTVglobemedia, which included the CTV and TSN networks. He was not keen to throw more billions around.

As it turned out, Cope and Mohamed cut a deal in late 2011 that was rooted in their fears the other guy would land MLSE by himself. This meant Rogers and Bell could split the regional broadcast rights for all of the MLSE teams evenly among their networks.

While the NHL was the outfit making hundreds of millions on the national broadcast rights of the Canadian teams, that only concerned about 30 games per season for each team. The other 52 games (with some teams this was as high as 60) were designated as regional games and each team could sell that package to the highest bidder. As the team that drew the highest television ratings by far, the Leafs' regional package, while not as lucrative as the Canadian national deal, still brought the team a lot more money than any other Canadian NHL team and just about every US-based team as well.

In the spring of 2007, well before the sale of MLSE, the Maple Leafs sold the rights to 30 of their regional games to Sportsnet, giving the Rogers network the exclusive rights to most of the regional package. The other 20 games were the property of MLSE's own cable station, Leafs TV. *The Globe and Mail* reported that Rogers landed the eight-year deal by agreeing to pay the Leafs $700,000 per game, a 56-per-cent increase from the $450,000 per game Sportsnet and Bell Media's TSN had been paying the team. The lengthy deal eventually meant Rogers and Bell had to wait until the end of the 2014–15 season to once again split the regional rights between them. By comparison, the second-best regional deal in the NHL in 2007 was the $300,000 per game Sportsnet paid the Vancouver Canucks. Vancouver is Canada's second-largest English-language market.

An interesting side deal of the MLSE purchase came to have a long-lasting effect on both TSN and Sportsnet. Multiple sources with knowledge of the terms of the sale said during their negotiations, Cope and Mohamed agreed they would charge the same subscription fee per customer to the carriers of the TSN and Sportsnet networks. This represented a nice jump in revenue for Sportsnet, as it lagged behind TSN in both subscribers and viewers since its inception in 1998. Since Bell and Rogers were also the biggest cable and satellite carriers in Canada, when they agreed to sell each other's sports networks to each other for the same price, the other carriers had to follow suit.

The new price represented a small increase in the price of subscriber fees for TSN but a much larger one for Sportsnet. By 2011, Sportsnet was just behind TSN in subscribers at just under nine million. But over the next three years it started losing them, falling to 8.3 million in 2014, about 700,000 behind TSN, which maintained its base at nine million despite all the cord-cutting. However, Sportsnet's revenue from its three main channels (Sportsnet, Sportsnet One, Sportsnet 360) grew from $148.2 million in 2011 to $220.3 million in 2014. That brought it just behind TSN, which went from $112.8 million in 2011 to $256.1 million in 2014, an eye-popping leap.

Even though the MLSE purchase gave Rogers equal control with Bell Canada of the most valuable sports properties in Canada to go with the Toronto Blue Jays, Edward and Melinda were not happy with the deal. They thought Mohamed should have bought the majority share of MLSE when he had the chance.

The MLSE deal was not the first time Bell Media, which owned TSN, RDS and CTV as its major broadcast properties, and Rogers Media, the Sportsnet owner, worked together. They formed a consortium along with the CBC to buy the Canadian rights to the 2010 Winter Olympics in Vancouver and the 2012 Summer Games in London. The group paid $153 million for both events and lost money on the deal, although how much is not known. It was enough for both of the big telecoms to opt out of being the main players in future bids, as they each took a lesser role when the CBC landed the rights for the Games, both winter and summer, from 2014 through 2024. With Bell and Rogers out of the bidding, the cost of those games was much lower.

Owning MLSE jointly was a much better proposition for Bell and Rogers than the Olympics. They even appeared to get along, at least in the first few years of their ownership. That was easy to do when raking in profits of more than $80 million per year from the Leafs alone.

However, the new partners shocked the hockey world shortly after the 2012–13 NHL lockout ended. As the league's 30 teams were preparing to begin a season shortened to 48 games, Toronto Maple Leafs GM Brian Burke was fired on January 9, 2013. No one saw it coming, including Burke.

"There's some times when you get fired and you see the vultures circling and you understand it's coming," Burke told reporters at his goodbye press conference. "You're not sure when you're going to drop dead in the desert, but it's coming and you can see the vultures.

"This one here was like a two-by-four upside the head to me."

As it turned out, however, Burke's departure was in the works for a while. The instigator, according to some media reports, was Bell Canada CEO George Cope. It was said Cope came to dislike Burke's loud, profane style and his many public disputes, mostly with the media. Cope didn't think it fit the corporate image of MLSE or its owners. While Cope is a physically imposing man and could be as bare-knuckled as Burke, according to those who know him, it is all done behind closed doors.

Sources close to either MLSE or BCE or both told reporters that Cope had been pushing to fire Burke for months. At some point, he convinced Mohamed to agree. Cope has never commented directly on his role in the firing. The long lobbying was necessary because the purchase agreement for MLSE stipulated Bell and Rogers would vote as one on company matters. This prevented Tanenbaum, with his 25-per-cent stake, from playing the two telecoms against each other.

The firing also made it clear Tanenbaum, who had come to operate as if MLSE were his company alone, no longer had silent partners who let him do as he pleased. Tanenbaum was opposed to firing Burke but he was outvoted by Cope, Mohamed and the other Rogers and Bell representatives on the MLSE board. Not only that, Tanenbaum was given the job, along with MLSE president Tom Anselmi and MLSE director Dale Lastman (Tanenbaum's lone ally on the board), of telling Burke he was finished.

Given that the Maple Leafs under Burke had a mediocre 128-135-42 record in slightly more than four years, his departure was not a total shock. But the timing was, since the shortened season was about to start. General managers are usually fired at or near the end of hockey seasons, so the new person can take stock of the franchise in the off-season. Leafs' director of hockey operations Dave Nonis, a Burke protegé who had already replaced him years earlier when the Vancouver Canucks fired Burke and was once again promoted to be his replacement, tried to talk his superiors into letting Burke at least finish the season. But their unhappiness was such that they wouldn't hear of it. Nonis may have been a disciple of Burke's on three NHL teams but his buttoned-down personality was the opposite of the mercurial Burke. Indeed, Nonis's most important job was often to convince Burke to pause for second thoughts on some impulsive move.

True to his nature, Burke did not go quietly, although he admitted when you don't have a winning record, your personality can become an issue for team owners.

"I can stand here and say it's my personality, they didn't like my personality, but those all become pretexts and excuses later," he said. "If you've won enough games, you can be as obnoxious as you want to be.

"The people that hired me hired Brian Burke. Maybe the new guys don't like that brand, maybe they want someone who is a little more conventional. They're entitled to that, that's fine. I'm not changing. I'm not going to change how I do things, that's not possible."

Things barely settled down with MLSE when Rogers delivered another shock. After announcing the fourth quarter of 2012 was one of the best in company history, Mohamed said he would step down in a year's time, in January 2014. Considering that in the same announcement Rogers said it would increase the company dividend by 10 per cent and buy back $500-million worth of shares thanks to a 30-per-cent jump in profits in the quarter to $455 million, Mohamed's departure came as an enormous surprise.

But there was trouble lurking behind those rosy numbers, not the least of which was an unhappy family of controlling shareholders. While Mohamed may have been a good counterbalance to the Ted Rogers era with his steady-as-she-goes style, this was not enough to satisfy Ted's old friends, who still populated the board and served on the family trust that controlled the voting shares. Edward and Melinda Rogers had the additional grievances of being shunted aside by Mohamed in the company hierarchy.

Mohamed might have been able to manage the discontent of the Rogers family and friends if his winning streaks, which started 10 years earlier, had continued. But by late 2012 Rogers lost its big lead in the wireless business to Bell and Telus. Rogers no longer seemed the nimble, fast-moving company of old. Bell Canada, once the slow-moving behemoth famous for its mediocre customer service and reluctance to change with the times, was now seen as the quick, aggressive force under Cope's leadership.

As it turned its focus away from television, now selling connections to the Internet to customers who cancelled their cable service, Rogers, which no longer had the iPhone market to itself, fell to third in the net additions of the lucrative post-paid subscribers. In the fourth quarter of 2012, Rogers had just 58,000 net account additions compared to 144,000 for Bell and 123,000 for Telus. Its post-paid churn rate, which shows how many wireless customers drop the company versus new subscribers, was the worst of the big three at 1.4 per cent. An additional kick in the pants was that Rogers lost 25,000 cable customers in the same period.

For his part, Mohamed insisted that he was not pushed out by the Rogers board or the family. "Absolutely, categorically my choice," he told *The Globe and Mail* shortly after the announcement. However, *Toronto Life* pointed to a move by Mohamed shortly after the sale of MLSE was completed that left company observers wondering if he precipitated his own departure.

When Mohamed was hired as CEO—like every other businessman would in his situation—he negotiated a golden parachute as part of his employment contract. This clause, which was nailed down tightly, said that if Mohamed and the Rogers board ever disagreed over his vision for the company he had the right to leave with a compensation package worth nearly $18 million. This was a canny move given the remaining influence of the Rogers family and Ted's old friends and the ongoing tension with Edward Rogers in particular.

Not long before his departure was announced, Mohamed appeared in front of the Rogers board and laid out his plans for the next five years. Part of this was a new structure for senior management. When neither Edward nor Melinda Rogers appeared on the organizational chart, it was easy to conclude Mohamed may have forced the board's hand. At that point, who was to say if he walked away with his $18 million or he was pushed?

When he announced his "retirement" in February 2013, Mohamed said he would step down a year later in February 2014, which meant he would have been in the top job at Rogers for just five years. He actually left in December 2013, just after the NHL contract was approved by the league's board of governors.

While Mohamed did not help his longevity by going slow on acquisitions, there was at least one company division that was still making the kind of deals that would have made Ted Rogers proud. Ever since he surprised the broadcast industry—not to mention his bosses at Bell Media—by quitting as president of Canada's Olympic broadcast consortium and as executive vice-president of strategic planning at CTV to become president of Rogers Media in August 2010, Keith Pelley was writing cheques to beef up the Rogers broadcasting and sports properties.

Pelley, whose enthusiasm for the things he feels passionate about is reflected in his rising manner of speech when he gets excited, was 46 when Rogers hired him but he had a wide-ranging resumé. After starting as an editorial assistant and then news producer at TSN in 1986, Pelley became president of the network by 2001 after a sojourn as an NFL producer with the Fox network. The restless Pelley, who never hesitates to follow his heart, gave up running the No. 1 sports television network in Canada to follow his passion for football, in this case the three-down variety.

In 2003, Pelley made what many considered a step down when he signed on as president of the Toronto Argonauts of the CFL. The Argos may be in Canada's largest city but they slipped badly in the affections of Toronto sports fans when the Blue Jays came along in 1977. Through most of the 1970s, the Argos drew crowds of more than 50,000 to Exhibition Stadium. But after the Argos won their first Grey Cup in 50 years in 1982, the crowds started to dwindle year by year until the average attendance for an Argo game was less than 30,000 by the time they moved to the SkyDome in 1989. By that time, it was the Blue Jays who were packing in the 50,000-plus fans for every game. Eventually, the Argo crowds were less than 20,000 per game. But Pelley was a huge Argo fan and he embraced the job with his usual energy until 2007 when he went back to Bell Media to run the Olympic consortium.

When Pelley bolted for Rogers Media in 2010, he soon brought in an old friend, Scott Moore, who left his post as head of both the CBC Sports and Revenue departments to become president of broadcasting under Pelley. Like Brian Burke and Dave Nonis, Pelley and Moore were opposites in temperament, although they were more equal colleagues rather than mentor and protegé.

Where Pelley was excitable and given to grand gestures, Moore was the measured one, preferring more discussion before making moves. Together they set about adding properties to Rogers Media to make a charge at top-dog Bell and its TSN property.

In September 2011, Pelley and Moore started *Sportsnet* magazine and one year later bought The Score, Canada's third sports television network. The Score morphed into Sportsnet 360 and became another national channel. In the same period, they also bought more than a dozen broadcasting properties for Sportsnet, among them the regional rights to five NHL teams, including the Maple Leafs. Rogers also bought sports properties like the Grand Slam of Curling that proved to be a good draw on television. Others included the Tour de France, international soccer and cricket, which were fringe sports for Canadian audiences in comparison to hockey and baseball.

The Blue Jays' payroll was bumped by $40 million for the 2013 season in the hope of creating a playoff team and reaping the TV ratings bonanza. That attempt failed but it did create a bigger payroll as the foundation for the unexpected success of the Blue Jays two years later. As a precursor to the NHL deal, perhaps, Moore boasted at the press conference leading into the 2013 Blue Jays season that *Sportsnet* magazine meant Rogers was now "the only five-platform sports brand in Canada. We have TV, radio, online, mobile and publishing, so we're able to do more with our sports content than anybody else in the country."

However, Rogers remained No. 2 to TSN in the still-important television fight and it had the publishing platform to itself because TSN was not in the field and had no interest in joining. TSN was also half-heartedly in the online platform battle and still held a big edge over its rival. Sportsnet hired a bunch of sportswriters away from their print employers to provide original content for their web site, Sportsnet.ca. But TSN.ca was simply used for wire-service stories, video clips from the network and scripts of what its stars like hockey commentators Bob McKenzie and Darren Dreger said earlier on television.

According to numbers compiled by the *Toronto Star*, TSN.ca drew 2.3 billion page views in 2012, easily the top sports web site in Canada despite its dearth of original content. A TSN executive, who would not speak on the record for obvious reasons, once admitted the company saw no reason to improve its web site by spending money on reporters and original content because it was No. 1 anyway. Finally, in 2014, TSN hired Rick Westhead as an investigative reporter and added Frank Seravalli as senior hockey writer a year later. Their work was intended for TSN.ca, although both spent a lot of time on television, particularly Westhead, who produced television stories in addition to web-site versions.

The Sportsnet personalities were also playing catch-up to their TSN counterparts on social media. By 2012, according to the *Toronto Star*, TSN's Bob McKenzie and Darren Dreger were among the most-followed of any Canadian media people on Twitter. McKenzie, regarded as the ultimate hockey insider by both Canadian and US fans, had 546,000 Twitter followers while Dreger had 413,845.

The work by Pelley and Moore produced ratings gains for Sportsnet. By 2013, the *Toronto Star* reported, Rogers' Sportsnet National and Sportsnet One networks were up 21 per cent over 2012. However, TSN still maintained a healthy ratings lead. TSN's average per-minute audience through May 2013 was 145,000 compared to 96,000 for Sportsnet.

When it came to radio, the companies were more evenly matched. While Rogers had the No. 1 sports-radio station in the country and in the biggest market with Toronto's Sportsnet 590 The Fan, with TSN 1050 Toronto far in the rear-view mirror, TSN had the leading stations in the other large Canadian cities except for Calgary.

With the NHL rights set to come up for negotiation in the summer and fall of 2013, Pelley believed the future of Sportsnet was at stake. Along with the NHL, TSN had other strong properties with a good chunk of NFL football, the CFL, the major tournaments in golf and tennis, US college football and lots of content from ESPN, which was a minority owner of TSN at the time. Pelley was worried that Sportsnet's weaker lineup of the Blue Jays, some regional NHL games, a share of the NFL and a few other lesser sports would not be enough to draw the ratings necessary to survive if it was shut out of the national NHL broadcasts.

"No question. You would meander in mediocrity and hoping every year the Blue Jays did well and the world curling tour took off," Pelley said. "All of a sudden all the NHL regional rights were going to be tougher and tougher to maintain.

"I hazard a guess if it had been reversed and TSN had acquired all the NHL rights, with our strength of schedule, then Sportsnet would have been relegated to a distant second in perpetuity. That was something we were totally aware of at the time. [TSN] already had great strength in terms of all of the properties they controlled, from the majors in tennis and golf. They were already dominant.

"What happened if they had taken the overall package? What would have happened to Sportsnet? You had the Blue Jays, some regional hockey, that's what was making up your schedule. What was a very dominant service in TSN would become even stronger.

"That was a conversation we knew. If TSN was to acquire this what happens to Sportsnet? It would be pretty detrimental, pretty dire if that happened."

This opinion was not shared by several competitors. A TSN executive, who declined to speak for attribution, said Sportsnet would have been just fine with that lineup because regional NHL hockey does well in the winter.

"The Blue Jays are a big piece. Basically that's 162 prime-time nights a year," the rival executive said. "This is a huge piece for you: they had regional hockey. Amazing contracts with regional hockey deals providing 50 games [per team] from those whole markets. The juiciest hockey content you could offer to those markets. This was not Pittsburgh–Nashville. It was Calgary and Edmonton and Vancouver [and Toronto] at the time."

Another rival executive said Sportsnet would have survived and even thrived because if Bell Media had won the national NHL contract it would have dropped all of its regional NHL contracts when they expired. The TSN bosses thought both the national and regional NHL contracts would have been too expensive and would also create a glut of hockey on their schedule. This would have allowed Sportsnet to practically name its price for the regional games of six of the Canadian teams aside from the Leafs.

Given TSN's varied lineup of programming it was no surprise its executives were confident Bell Media was the only company suited for taking over the NHL's national Canadian rights despite one of their number's kind words for Sportsnet. In addition to TSN, Bell could rival the CBC in over-the-air television reach as it owned the CTV network. Rogers did not have anything comparable, as its City network was just in the major cities in Canada and its presence in Atlantic Canada was limited. Bell also owned a French network in RDS, while Rogers did not.

Phil King, a refreshingly colourful TV executive, was then president of CTV and sports programming for Bell, which meant he was in charge of TSN. King did not want to discuss the competition in detail but he was willing to admit Pelley and Moore caught TSN's attention with their programming moves.

"I think we're the undisputed heavyweight champion, going on 27 years," King told the *Toronto Star*. "There's no doubt there's someone nipping at our heels. I don't want to talk about our competitors but there's no doubt we've had to sharpen our game somewhat.

"They've decided to make a real game of it. I'm not so sure that the first 15 years [after Sportsnet was founded in 1998] were much of a game, frankly, but it's more of a game the last three. But we still have an enviable position."

Certainly when it came to hockey, TSN was in an enviable position. It held a national contract with the NHL that gave it 70 regular-season games and two rounds of playoff games. The network also had the Montreal Canadiens' English and French regional rights as well as the Winnipeg Jets' regional contract. And there was a world junior hockey championship, which dominated the Canadian sports TV ratings from Christmas through the new year, as long as Canada was in contention. On top of all the games, TSN's hockey shows led the ratings. The panel shows with broadcasters like James Duthie, Bob McKenzie, Darren Dreger, Aaron Ward and Pierre LeBrun were the most-watched of their kind.

By this time, the senior managers at TSN had a reputation among their peers at the other networks of being a little cocky. Given the network's lead in the overall numbers, perhaps they could not be blamed, although this attitude was to be cited down the road after the NHL negotiations played out. By early 2011, for example, TSN's average audience per minute was 178,000 viewers. That was more than double Sportsnet's 87,000.

Over at the CBC, there was a sense of foreboding rather than excitement when it came to the prospects of hanging on to *Hockey Night in Canada*. By the spring of 2013, shortly before the CBC's exclusive negotiating period with the NHL was to begin, the network had spent the past year absorbing the budget cuts forced on it by the Harper government.

Management was on its way to cutting a planned 650 jobs, a number that was sure to grow if the NHL contract was lost. Those 650 jobs were the second round of layoffs in recent years for the CBC. In 2009, management said it planned to eliminate 800 jobs when the federal government refused to cover a $65-million short-fall in the CBC's annual budget. The total was lower, although an exact number is not known because many workers took early-retirement offers or buyouts. But the cuts didn't end there. Along with the jobs, two foreign news bureaus were closed and 175 hours of original programming were chopped, which included documentaries, radio and television current-affairs shows as well as sports programs.

The sense of doom may have been confined to the rank-and-file workers as the NHL negotiations approached in 2013. Outwardly, at least, the executives at the top of the network expressed hope they would be able to work out a new deal with the NHL even as they were cutting budgets.

A *Globe and Mail* story quoted network president Hubert Lacroix telling CBC employees in 2012 that hockey remained a priority because of the advertising revenue it attracted. Since an exact number is not revealed in the CBC financial statements, estimates of the annual hockey advertising revenue ranged from $130 million to $225 million. But it is known hockey was the single biggest portion of the advertising revenue, although CBC executives had long said it was no longer the money-spinner it used to be thanks to the rising cost of NHL rights fees, which were $105 million in 2013–14, the last year of the CBC deal.

"I don't think this is going to be easy," Lacroix told the CBC employees of the chances of keeping *Hockey Night*. "I think we have a good relationship [with the NHL] and some of the choices we're making are to ensure we have the means necessary to put a really credible offer on the table."

Lacroix was appointed president of the CBC in November 2007 by the Harper government. But he had little experience in broadcasting, aside from stints with Radio-Canada as a basketball commentator at three Olympics thanks to his sideline as a coach. Lacroix spent most of his working life as a corporate lawyer and law professor and he was regarded by many CBC employees as a political appointee by the federal Conservatives. Lacroix resented this description and in his defence it must be noted that practically from the day he started his job he had to deal with a series of funding cuts by the government.

The signs leading up to the negotiations were not good. Jeffrey Orridge was hired in January 2011 to replace Scott Moore as the head of CBC Sports. One of Orridge's most important duties was to negotiate broadcast deals with the governing bodies of sports. In the months leading up to the NHL negotiations, the CBC's precarious financial position was reflected in a series of rights losses, although Orridge could not be blamed for this because the public corporation simply did not have the money.

There were hopes the CBC would be able to regain a portion of the CFL rights when they came up for renewal in 2013. But TSN, perhaps spooked by Rogers' increasing activity in buying sports properties, renewed its exclusive deal with the CFL at more than double the previous one to an average of $38 million per year. Then the CBC lost soccer's World Cup when TSN outbid it for the FIFA package for seven years beginning in 2015. But there was one victory for Orridge—he and Kirstine Stewart, head of CBC's English services, landed the 2014 Sochi Games and the 2016 Rio de Janeiro Games with a $90-million bid. They also signed up Bell and Rogers as partners.

While the CBC landed the two Olympics only because Bell and Rogers declined to bid after losing money on the $153 million they collectively paid as a consortium for the Vancouver and London Olympics in 2010 and 2012, the partnership was a good sign. By 2013, the conventional wisdom in the broadcast industry was that the only way the CBC would survive as an NHL rights-holder would be to partner with either of the two telecom giants. The public network had the field to itself as a partner since the MLSE purchase agreement between Rogers and Bell and the NHL stipulated they could not become partners in any bid for the NHL's broadcast rights. This was to head off any collusion between the two giants in order to keep the price down.

However, as the CBC's exclusive negotiating period approached in the summer, it began to appear as if the public network was planning to go it alone. "They thought they could keep *Hockey Night* pretty much on the terms they had it," said Scott Moore, who maintained close relationships with a lot of CBC people after he left for Rogers. "Whether that's naïve or not …"

3

SETTING THE STAGE

While the media industry was worrying about declining viewers, readers, listeners, cable subscriptions and broadcast and print advertising in the spring of 2013, the NHL was thinking a nice bump in revenue was just around the corner. NHL commissioner Gary Bettman and John Collins, the league's chief operating officer and head of marketing, who would negotiate the next national Canadian broadcast contract, were well aware of conventional television's problems. By this time ESPN, controlled by the Walt Disney Company along with ABC, was feeling the first pinch of being caught in the vise of cord-cutters and rising rights fees. It was a trend that would continue to this day, exacerbated by the slow response of media companies to the problem, with ESPN being the best example.

In 2011, ESPN was seen in 100 million US homes on either cable or satellite services, according to Nielsen, the leading ratings company. But that was the peak for the network. The numbers began to slide in 2012 as the popularity of streaming video took hold and cable and pay-TV subscriptions were cancelled.

None of this was the NHL's concern as Bettman and Collins prepared for the negotiations. They knew they were in for a big score simply because the big dogs—Bell and Rogers—were probably going to spend like never before. In previous years, there were always threats that either or both of the telecoms would take away *Hockey Night in Canada* from the CBC, but they never did. Now, though, the competition between Bell and Rogers and their sports networks was heating up because so much was at stake. With the broadcast industry under attack due to eroding viewership, the fact that sports programming could still hold its own because the best of it was live meant neither company wanted to let the other get a step up by grabbing the most popular sport in Canada.

"The NHL is the most important content in the country, not unlike the NFL in the United States," said Collins, who spent most of his career in the NFL before coming to the NHL in 2006. "We thought we had a lot more leverage [than in the previous contract] and a lot greater opportunity, both in terms of coverage as well as financial opportunity."

By 2013, Gary Bettman was in his 20th year as commissioner of the NHL. In those 20 years he took the NHL from a mom-and-pop business that pulled in revenues of $732 million (US) in his first season on the job to $3.3 billion in 2011–12, just before the third lockout during Bettman's tenure. Revenues hit $3.7 billion in 2013–14, the first full season after the 2012–13 lockout. While Bettman and the owners stoutly argue the lockouts were necessary to gain economic stability, primarily with the forced introduction of a salary cap in 2005, the labour woes are considered one of the few major blights (the concussion and CTE issue being the other one) on his generally excellent record as commissioner. Bettman can also argue player salaries went from an average of $558,000 (US) in 1993–94 to $2.55 million in the same period league revenues went up more than four-fold.

Bettman did not achieve this by operating by the seat of his pants. Aside from his reputation as a smart, merciless negotiator, Bettman was known as a careful planner who sussed out every possibility in a course of action. That meant a team of executives under Bettman and Collins spent the year leading up to the opening of negotiations with the CBC analyzing the situation. Everything from potential financial opportunities from the newer digital platforms to areas where the networks could improve their coverage of the league was examined (building the profiles of the players, long a Bettman favourite, was a big item).

Bettman and Collins had already been through the same process a few years earlier when the $2-billion contract with NBC was landed in 2011. One of the key findings in that process was that emphasis on the playoffs needed to be made on US television. Collins said the main thing they wanted to fix was the blackout problem where the regional rights-holders in the US held sway over the national broadcaster and the national broadcast was not shown in the cities of the two participating teams in each playoff series. Back in 1994, this led to an embarrassing situation in the Stanley Cup final when the New York Rangers finally won the NHL championship after a 54-year drought. Having the team that represented North America's largest media market make the Stanley Cup final after such a long absence was a huge boon for the NHL, which always struggled to shake its image as a regional attraction in the US. But promoting the league to that huge audience took a hit because the US rights contract in place at the time called for ESPN, the national broadcaster, to be blacked out in New York for the Rangers' home games in favour of the team's local broadcaster, the MSG pay network, which was seen in far fewer homes. So a lot fewer people than expected saw the Rangers win their first Cup since 1940 on home ice.

By the next season, Bettman had the television problem in hand, having surprised most who follow the NHL by securing a national US contract with a major over-the-air network. Fox broadcast two games of the 1995 Stanley Cup final, splitting what turned out to be a four-game sweep for the New Jersey Devils over the Detroit Red Wings with ESPN, the league's cable broadcaster. It was the first time a Cup final game was shown on a major over-the-air US network since 1980. Bettman won the job as commissioner by promising to spread the NHL's presence around the US through expansion in order to get that elusive major US television contract. Landing Fox was the first major accomplishment of Bettman's career. The first Fox deal was worth only $155 million (US) but the size of both the contracts and the NHL have gone up since then.

One of the conclusions reached by Bettman and Collins was that like the US a few years earlier, more promotion was needed in Canada for the NHL playoffs. Yes, the games dominated the schedules of CBC and TSN for more than two months every spring, but they thought the CBC in particular could do more to promote the playoffs on its other shows and other platforms. Bettman and Collins saw the NHL playoffs as the Canadian equivalent of the NCAA basketball tournament, which drew all kinds of attention in March every year and caught up even casual fans due to the popularity of the bracket pools.

"We were saying, 'Look, we're going to make the playoffs a real platform," Collins said. "Hopefully equal to March Madness and promote the hell out of it for six weeks.'"

Another goal was to turn Sunday night into a *Hockey Night* for Canadians along with the traditional Saturday night broadcasts. Collins, the old NFL hand, thought the NHL could spread itself around just like his former league did by expanding beyond the traditional Sunday-afternoon schedule to Monday nights, then Sunday nights and, finally, Thursday nights. "There was a lot of time spent, a lot of work and a lot of thought as to how we saw it. We saw Sunday night as a real opportunity," Collins said.

The NHL bosses also thought Saturday night itself could stand a lot of improvement. This may sound strange considering *Hockey Night in Canada* had been a Canadian institution since 1952 but Collins and Bettman thought there was much to be done. Their biggest complaint about the CBC's production on Saturday nights was that there weren't enough games on television. *Hockey Night* ran doubleheaders every Saturday night, generally with an eastern team featured in the first game, which started at 7 p.m. Eastern time, and a western team in the second game, which would start at 10 p.m. But CBC divided the country into viewing zones for each team and only two games per night would be seen in each zone. For example, in Toronto and Southern Ontario, viewers would get the Toronto Maple Leafs' game since it was the home team in that zone plus a game with at least one of the western teams like the Canucks, Oilers or Flames. The only time those viewers did not get a Leafs game was if the team had a rare Saturday night off. If the Leafs were on a western road trip, their game was usually the second game of the doubleheader and people saw the Ottawa Senators or Montreal Canadiens in the first game.

But the viewers were not able to watch any more than two games on the CBC. If the Senators were playing at the same time as the Maple Leafs, for example, their game was blacked out in Southern Ontario. The only way to see more games was to buy the NHL's pay-TV package. This made as much sense to Bettman and Collins as Game 7 of the 1994 Stanley Cup final being blacked out in New York on ESPN.

"We talked about Saturday night, the busiest night in the league for hockey, and yet in the most passionate market in the world for hockey you're showing two games," Collins said. "There had to be a way to make all the other games around the league available for the fans that wanted it. We felt like that was a huge opportunity for us and the CBC could no longer insist on two games and black everything out, including all our digital platforms. It was like analogue in a digital world. It just didn't fly anymore."

Collins also saw *Hockey Night* in the same terms as many observers did, a beloved institution that was uniquely Canadian, which gave it great power as an advertising vehicle. Companies who placed commercials on the Saturday night show were putting their product in front of entire families.

"There was nothing like *Hockey Night in Canada*," Collins said. "You talk about *Monday Night Football* in the US, but in its glory days I don't think it had the cultural relevance that hockey means in Canada, what *Hockey Night* meant on Saturday nights for the entire family.

"*Monday Night Football* was special but it was a different kind of special. It was guys' night out sitting in a bar, watching the game. *Hockey Night* was a family sitting down together, a unifying force."

Most of the NHL's analysis and preparation for the negotiations were done on the assumption the Canadian national contract would continue under the old model of multiple networks on multiple nights. In the existing deal, which expired after the 2013–14 season, the CBC had Saturday nights while TSN did its national broadcasts on Wednesday nights. There were a few exceptions, where each network would show an important game on another night, but that was the general schedule. It was also why Collins and Bettman could contemplate opening Saturday night to more than two games and more than just the CBC as a broadcaster without cutting too deeply into the sale of NHL Centre Ice, the league's pay package. The NHL has always designated certain nights of the week for national broadcasts, in this case Wednesday and Saturday, with Sunday added as part of the new deal in 2014. This left the other nights of the week open for the pay package. Also, the home team's games were blacked out on Centre Ice in each market, so they were never part of the deal anyway.

As the negotiating period drew near, the idea that the NHL would continue with more than one broadcast partner took hold among those in and around the NHL community. The assumption was that CBC would either find the money to pay almost double the existing annual fee ($200 million was the consensus) for a Saturday night package or it would work out a partnership with one of the big players, likely Bell Media. Then Bell Media would pay its own huge fee for the Wednesday nights it already had plus another night, with Rogers coming in for another whack of money to take over Sundays. The digital rights would likely go to either Bell or Rogers.

The NHL negotiators kicked around a great number of ideas, including those, but did not tie themselves to anything. There was another approach to how the rights would be packaged that Bettman and Collins found intriguing but one that had yet to be tried by any of the major North American sports leagues. They called this the "gatekeeper" model. This was the notion that all of the NHL's broadcast rights—television, radio, digital and mobile—would be sold to one company. While the buyer would have the right to sell off parts of the deal, such as games it did not want to accommodate on its schedule, the idea was that this company would be large enough and have the infrastructure to handle all of the platforms. Hence the gatekeeper moniker; if you wanted access to the NHL, you had to go through this company.

"The first option was to 'slice and dice' as Gary [Bettman] liked to say," Collins said. "We would try to create these individual packages and try to get maximum value for these packages and ultimately have more people engaged with NHL hockey than we had before. Everybody would be spending their production dollars and promotion dollars making the game even bigger. That was the first option.

"If we weren't going to get maximum value for that, then the other option was to go with the gatekeeper model. That's where we offer exclusive rights for all the content with a view towards being able to maximize distribution by letting that gatekeeper figure out how. Now you're talking a subscription for mobility, digital distribution. But the gatekeeper model we saw as a second option to try and capture the value we saw in the marketplace."

While he wouldn't say as much, chances are Collins thought the gatekeeper model was designed with Bell Media in mind. At least the Rogers guys, Keith Pelley and Scott Moore, thought so. After all, Bell had the infrastructure in place that Rogers did not. In addition to TSN, Bell owned CTV, which rivalled the CBC for over-the-air reach in Canada. Rogers had the wireless and digital capability to match Bell, along with the Sportsnet network, but it did not have anything to compare with CTV.

At this point, the Bell people felt confident they would be able to maintain their grip on at least a large piece of the national rights and probably expand their hold. The CBC's financial woes meant it would be fortunate to hang on to some version of *Hockey Night*. As for Rogers, the TSN executives regarded it as a competitor but when the talks came to the serious question of money and services they thought they had more to offer the NHL. Once the CBC's exclusive negotiating period was over on September 1, the Bell people thought, TSN should be able to nail down the lion's share of the contract.

Rogers managed to carve out an interesting position for itself as the summer of 2013 wound down and the period when the NHL would solicit bids from outside the CBC approached. While Rogers Media president Keith Pelley and president of broadcasting Scott Moore were eager to chase the NHL rights, they let it be known in the broadcasting industry they were not sure about bidding on the package. They felt their chances were better if they came in as a surprise late in the bidding. So people were told that because Rogers was about to change CEOs from Nadir Mohamed (who would step down in December) to British telecom executive Guy

Laurence they might not be able to make a billion-dollar deal like that one.

"One of the secrets of the negotiation and why we took everybody by surprise is we messaged out to a lot of people in the industry that, hey, we're in transition, we don't know if we'll be able to make a bid," Moore said. "So everybody just assumed we would not be a bidder. That was absolutely part of the strategy."

By the time negotiations began between the CBC and the NHL, their relationship was a far cry from what it was when the existing deal began in 2007. That was also the year Moore became head of CBC Sports, although he did not have a hand in negotiating the NHL broadcast contract, which began in the 2007–08 season and ran to the end of 2013–14. When Moore took over at CBC he worked hard to establish a rapport with the Canadian NHL teams. He held meetings with the presidents of the six Canadian teams every year at the all-star game starting in 2008.

"I was shocked the Canadian teams had never met as a group in the same room," Moore said. "We talked about things like how to market to ethnic communities, how to work together to maximize the ratings on *Hockey Night*, promotions we could do together."

Collins was in his second year with the NHL when these meetings started and he raised an eyebrow when he discovered they were only for the CBC and the Canadian teams. League executives like him were not invited.

"They would talk about their business issues, talent, whatever they needed to do," Collins said. "They would put together a little agenda for the Canadian clubs [and] the Canadian rightsholder to gather the power, the momentum to take on the league on certain issues. The Canadian business issues were very often different than the US business issues. It was an unusual way of doing it."

This doesn't mean the Canadian teams and Moore were at loggerheads with the NHL head office. Eventually Collins was invited to take part in the meetings. "I was a big proponent of Scott's. They were network partners. If they were having issues, we could help. We wanted to help," Collins said.

The advantage for Moore was the meetings helped him forge strong friendships with team executives like Roy Mlakar, who was then president of the Ottawa Senators; Calgary Flames president Ken King; Pat LaForge, who was president of the Edmonton Oilers at the time; and Tom Anselmi, then the chief operating officer of MLSE, who later became president of the Senators. Moore also became friends with Bettman and Collins. These relationships not only kept things smooth for a long time between the league and at least some departments of the CBC, they were a big help years later for Moore when Rogers came courting the NHL contract.

Things were not always so idyllic when it came to the relationships between Bettman and the higher levels of the CBC. Richard Stursberg was the CBC's head of English services before he was fired in 2010 and replaced by Kirstine Stewart. He was a hugely unpopular figure, by his own admission, mostly because he tried to turn the CBC away from its long-time emphasis on public-affairs and cultural programming to more commercial fare like *Dragons' Den* and *Battle of the Blades* in order to raise ratings. Even Stursberg described himself as "difficult, arrogant and often insubordinate," in his 2012 book about his six controversial years at the CBC, *The Tower of Babble*. Also in the book, Stursberg describes the *Hockey Night in Canada* negotiations for the previous NHL deal with Gary Bettman and deputy commissioner Bill Daly that stretched over 2006 and into 2007.

Two things jump out from that description: Stursberg's astonishing condescension toward Bettman and Daly and how utterly unprepared Stursberg and his fellow CBC executives were to negotiate with two whip-smart people who were far more skilled than they at making a deal. Even though it is Stursberg's side of the story, it comes through loud and clear that Bettman and Daly ran circles around him and then CBC president Robert Rabinovitch.

Like Jeffrey Orridge would several years later, Stursberg went into the negotiations with Bettman in April 2006 following a string of rights losses. But in this case, only one of the losses Stursberg presided over was strictly due to the CBC's worsening financial situation. First came the Olympics in 2005, when the Bell-Rogers consortium outbid the CBC and its partners for the 2010 and 2012 Games by a wide margin. Then CBC lost the rights to the Brier and the Scott Tournament of Hearts, the Canadian men's and women's curling championships. That was a competence issue rather than a money issue because the CBC made such a hash of broadcasting the 2005 championships, spreading important games around to obscure cable channels, that the Canadian Curling Association essentially forced the network to give up the contract. Finally, as the negotiations with Bettman were going on, TSN was able to wrest away the CBC's majority share of the CFL rights because the network's relationship with the league was beyond repair.

Stursberg decided to try to open the negotiations early on the next NHL contract, which expired after the 2006–07 season, because of two fears. One was that political pressure in Ottawa posed by the funding cuts would force the CBC to get out of the professional sports business and the other was that CTV and TSN would outbid the CBC for the NHL rights. Stursberg hoped to get a quick deal out of Bettman to head off both of those things. No one who knew the first thing about Bettman would have even considered the possibility. NHL executives say Bettman has always considered the CBC important to the NHL and wanted it to remain a partner in some form even if it could no longer afford a major stake in the television rights. But even those who know Bettman only slightly know he can never be pushed into anything, especially something that might not be the best possible business deal for his league. It seems not to have occurred to Stursberg that Bettman came to the negotiations fresh from sacrificing an entire NHL season in order to get a salary cap for his owners.

Nevertheless, Stursberg hoped to persuade Bettman that if he did not sign quickly with the CBC, the network might be forced out of bidding for major sports properties, leaving Bell Media as the only perceived other bidder, in position to lowball the NHL. The way Stursberg tells it, he and Rabinovitch and Nancy Lee, Moore's predecessor as head of CBC Sports, did a lot of research on the business model of *Hockey Night*. But there was no mention of any study of Bettman and Daly, their tactics, their history or their style of negotiating.

In describing the first meeting in April 2006 between himself and Rabinovitch, Bettman and Daly at a tony Manhattan restaurant favoured by celebrities, Stursberg's sneering comes on strong from the printed page. Stursberg does allow Bettman is an "extremely clever businessman" and both he and Daly love to negotiate. Then he describes Bettman as starstruck by the presence of famous people in the restaurant, like boxer Sugar Ray Leonard. Stursberg acknowledges Daly's reputation as the more personable of the NHL bosses but draws a picture of him as Bettman's enforcer. Daly, a beefy fellow with a shaved head, "looks like a menacing professional wrestler," according to Stursberg. Daly is never quoted as saying anything in any of their meetings, only staring at Stursberg "balefully," or glowering "menacingly."

To anyone who has ever met Daly, who became deputy commissioner of the NHL in 2005 at the age of 41, Stursberg's characterization of him is laughable. He may be a tough negotiator like Bettman but there is a softer side that is usually not far from the surface. The deputy commissioner is an Ivy League grad and a lawyer by trade but that has not prevented him from being a down-to-earth guy who loves to talk about his beloved Miami Dolphins over a beer or two. Daly's love for football comes honestly, as the New Jersey native was a running back for Dartmouth College in the 1980s. His love of hockey comes from his mother's side of the family. She is from Saskatoon.

Stursberg says he and his negotiating team went into the talks "confident that we knew much more than the NHL about advertising revenue and sports production costs. This was, after all, our business, not theirs. If we could not win on our own turf, we should hang up our skates and retire from the rink forever." As it turned out, they did not know more than Bettman about the broadcasting business. Bettman kept the CBC dangling for months, tantalizing them with the possibility that Bell might be whispering in his ear. Stursberg finally broke down and presented Bettman and Daly an offer. Bettman countered with a revenue model of the CBC he had commissioned. Stursberg protested Bettman's revenue numbers were "absurd to us." Bettman said the CBC's advertising prices were too low.

Months later, after Stursberg says he refused to give up more playoff games and Leafs games to TSN as well as the digital and wireless rights, Bettman agreed to a deal with the CBC. It was, according to Stursberg, the richest deal in Canadian sports history. He did not mention the money, only that the annual payments increased in the later years of the deal. Other sources said the contract topped out at $105 million in 2006–07, the final year. Stursberg did write that he agreed to the deal, which was expected to be profitable, in part because "although we would never admit it to Gary, our advertising rates were underpriced."

When Moore took over at CBC Sports in 2007, he worked hard to improve the relationship between the NHL and the network. As he came to know Bettman, Moore realized the commissioner had an acute sense of the importance of himself and the league. The NHL may have been far behind the NFL in terms of revenue and popularity but Bettman believed he and his colleagues should not be treated any differently in major negotiations than the commissioner of the NFL was. That meant the most important person in the company came to the bargaining table—Rupert Murdoch in the case of Fox when it was seeking the NFL rights— and took an active and respectful part in the talks.

While Moore made headway in the relations with the NHL, things began to slide after he left the CBC to join Pelley at Rogers in November 2010, not long after Stursberg was fired. Kirstine Stewart, who spent nearly two decades working in the film and television industries before joining the CBC, was promoted from her post as general manager to replace Stursberg. During her time as head of CBC's English-language services she had a good working relationship with Bettman, Daly and Collins. But Stewart left most of the NHL dealings to the sports people, including Jeffrey Orridge, whom she hired in April 2011 to replace Moore as the boss of CBC Sports.

By 2013, things deteriorated between the CBC and the NHL although it was not due to any antagonism with Orridge or Neil McEneaney, who was the interim replacement for Stewart, who left the CBC in the spring of 2013 for a job with Twitter. The tensions were building through *Hockey Night in Canada*, where Ron MacLean and Don Cherry were seen by the Leafs and other teams as unfair in their criticism and where there was a growing unhappiness with the show's emphasis on its own personalities instead of the league's players.

The fact that Orridge and McEneaney were both new to dealing with the NHL did not help, although Orridge knew Bettman well. Orridge, a native of New York City and a Harvard Law School grad, became general counsel for USA Basketball, the sport's governing body in the US, in 1991. Bettman had the same title with the NBA then, the No. 3 job in the league behind commissioner David Stern. Orridge and Bettman worked together on the joint marketing and licensing venture between their organizations before Bettman became commissioner of the NHL in February 1993.

However, what became a problem in the negotiations for the CBC went further up than Orridge and McEneaney. Hubert Lacroix, who was appointed CBC president in November 2007 by the Harper government, did not take part in the NHL negotiations in the summer of 2013. This did not go over well with Bettman, according to several sources.

A little later in 2013, after the CBC's exclusive negotiating period was over, BCE CEO George Cope made the same decision as Lacroix. This was not enough to derail the chances of either the CBC or Bell of landing the NHL rights but it was far from helpful for either company's cause. Both would have reason to regret the moves in the coming months.

4

TRYING TO MAINTAIN THE STATUS QUO

While the CBC negotiating team of McEneaney and Orridge were in discussions with Bettman and Collins in the summer of 2013, the executive team at Bell Media was doing its own planning. Phil King, then the president of CTV and sports programming, and Bell Media president Kevin Crull would handle the negotiations with Bettman and Collins with input from TSN president Stewart Johnston. King was well known in the broadcast business as an outspoken advocate for Bell who was not afraid to launch criticism at his rivals, often in a humorous way. Johnston and Crull, on the other hand, were more traditional executives who were cautious in their public pronouncements.

King, Crull, Johnston and their colleagues discussed all the possibilities of a new contract, including the gatekeeper and multi-network models. While Bell was interested in buying a gatekeeper contract, it was not committed to putting a lot of games on CTV, especially during the playoffs. The Bell executives did not see the value in disrupting CTV's profitable prime-time schedule for eight weeks in the spring during the playoffs. So the preference was for the multi-night, multi-network version of the deal and the possibility of a sub-licensing deal with the CBC, probably for Saturday nights. Rogers was not perceived as a big threat because the Bell team thought their rival would buy a Sunday-night package from the NHL.

Two sources close to Bell Media's leadership said they wanted to keep the CBC in the game if they won the contract. A number of scenarios were thrown around, from one night a week with two games to one game per week that alternated between east and west. However, the sources insisted, Bell Media would not have forced the same deal on the CBC that Rogers did, collecting all the advertising revenue, getting free office and studio space plus the CBC's technical staff in exchange for two games per week.

The way Bell saw it, that was taking on all the risk of being able to sell out the advertising time for both games. Bell would have done a traditional deal where the games would have been sold to the CBC for cash with the CBC then selling and running its own commercials during the games. Bell also thought that if it could form an official partnership with the CBC in a multi-network scenario, it would keep the price down.

It was with that in mind that Phil King approached Jeffrey Orridge early in the process. King knew the CBC could not afford the kind of money Bettman and Collins were after and on the TSN/CTV side of things, King and company did not want the number of games that would come with the extensive national package the NHL had in mind. In fact, if Bell Media landed the deal there were thoughts of shedding the existing regional rights packages of the teams TSN had as they expired. Under the multi-network model, there appeared to be the assumption TSN would get more midweek games, more playoff games, perhaps some Saturday games, with the CBC keeping one or two, and Sunday nights would go to Rogers.

King designed a plan based on the NCAA basketball tournament contract, which is shared by CBS, an over-the-air network, and Turner Sports, which owns the TBS and TNT cable networks. CBS and Turner split the March Madness games and they alternate showing the championship games on their networks each year. This way, viewers would be forced to keep their TSN cable packages because the big game would only be on regular TV every other year.

King told Orridge the CBC would get at least one game every Saturday for *Hockey Night in Canada*, perhaps two. He also said the public network could no longer count on showing the Maple Leafs every Saturday night. Their games would be evenly split with the Leafs playing more midweek games to benefit TSN's ratings. The playoffs would be split 50-50 with TSN getting access to the Stanley Cup final for the first time. At this point, King's proposal was more of an outline, with the details to be worked out as they went along. He figured the Cup final would either rotate between the networks, as NCAA basketball did in the US, or TSN might show the first two games of the NHL championship with the CBC carrying the rest.

What King also told Orridge was that the CBC would no longer be the lead partner on Saturday night, but that was inevitable given the money Bell, and probably Rogers, was prepared to throw at the NHL. King told Orridge that he should talk to CBC president Hubert Lacroix about his proposal, that it was time to put egos aside and take advantage of the opportunity to stay involved in the hockey broadcasts. The way King saw it, if both Bell and CBC approached Bettman and Collins as official partners they could force the NHL to give them a lower price than if they were pseudo-competitors.

However, King's pitch did not go any further. "I'm not aware of any conversations between Jeffrey Orridge and Phil King," Lacroix said.

Around the same time, Rogers Media also approached the CBC. Keith Pelley said the discussion was about "partnering, putting together a package in terms of us doing a package with them." The gatekeeper model was also discussed but Pelley said the CBC people "didn't believe the gatekeeper model would happen." If Rogers was going to get in on the action, it would need an over-the-air partner, especially if more than Sunday night was involved, so the CBC was the logical choice.

But that partnership pitch went nowhere, too, as the CBC went into its exclusive negotiating period looking for its own deal, hoping its record as a good partner of the NHL going back 60 years would provide some traction. The trouble was, while Bettman felt the CBC should remain part of the hockey broadcasts he didn't think it should be done at a cut-rate price.

When it came to the gatekeeper model, the Bell people were confident they were the only company in position to deliver on it. They had the conventional network in CTV that Rogers lacked, plus the TSN cable network and the digital and wireless capabilities as well as a French network in RDS.

Over at Rogers, Pelley, Moore and their team lay low, studying their options but not drawing any attention to themselves. In the end, it seems, they were taken too lightly not only by Bell Media but also by the CBC, which never saw Rogers coming until it was too late.

The CBC kicked off its campaign for the NHL rights with a breakfast meeting that involved network president Hubert Lacroix, Bettman and Collins. This seemed the right thing to do, making sure the top person at the network was front and centre with Bettman, who considered this no less than his due. There was some common ground between Bettman and Lacroix, as both had backgrounds as corporate lawyers. The meeting was cordial enough but by the end of it, the CBC's hopes, unbeknownst to it, were badly damaged. One NHL source familiar with the meeting said it was a bigger turning point in the CBC's eventual loss of the rights than the 2012 meeting of the NHL's board of governors at the Ottawa all-star game.

Bettman and Collins laid out in broad terms the kind of deal they were looking for. The gatekeeper model was not part of the discussions, since the CBC clearly did not have that kind of money, but Lacroix was told what the NHL was looking for in the new deal: more nights for national broadcasts, more availability on digital and mobile services, more cross-promotion on different platforms, more games shown on Saturday nights and a new focus on telling players' stories.

Lacroix did not reject any of the ideas, but Collins and Bettman felt he did not show a keen interest, either. Worst of all, Bettman and Collins thought he essentially told them hey, let me know what I can do but things are in good hands and I'll see you at the press conference when we announce the new contract. Collins was astonished and came away thinking he and Bettman were almost being trifled with, according to an NHL source. They felt the overall leader of the CBC should have become deeply involved in the talks with them. Collins thought Lacroix should have said these rights are the most important thing for the network and we need to make sure we keep them so let's work together, figure out what we each need and do it. Instead, it was, okay, we'll let you know what we can do. It was the last time Lacroix and Bettman would have a discussion until November 21, 2013, the day the commissioner called him to say the CBC was out, the NHL rights now belonged to Rogers, and Lacroix and company could expect a call from them.

Once it was clear Lacroix was not going to take an active role in the talks, said a source familiar with how Collins and Bettman were thinking at the time, the possibility the relationship between the NHL and the CBC was finished emerged for the first time.

"[Bettman and Collins] said this is the way we're thinking about it," the source said. "I don't think it was evolutionary, it was revolutionary. We're starting [negotiations] with you, not because there's a right of first negotiation but it's the right thing to do. It's the CBC, it's *Hockey Night*, let's build from there. And [they] got met with okay, we'll get back to you."

Lacroix argued that he did indeed have a keen interest in the talks. He said that in May 2013, Bettman appeared before the CBC's board of directors and told them he put a high value on the network's relationship with the NHL. While Lacroix admittedly did not have direct contact with Bettman over the summer of 2013, he said he was in constant contact with Orridge and McEneaney about the negotiations. Lacroix said he had confidence in his negotiating team, particularly because McEneaney played an important behind-the-scenes role in the 2006 negotiations for the previous contract, which were led by former CBC English services head Richard Stursberg.

There is no doubt the NHL rights were considered the most important property for the CBC by lots of management people. The rising cost of the rights combined with the continuing mediocrity of the Toronto Maple Leafs, who had not made the playoffs since 2004, greatly reduced *Hockey Night in Canada*'s profitability in recent years. But the show was still the network's biggest money-maker. In his book *Tower Of Babble*, Stursberg said *Hockey Night* "generated tens of millions of dollars for the corporation."

Stursberg wrote that, at the time, losing the NHL rights would cost the CBC between $240 million and $300 million. He estimated *Hockey Night* represented 400 hours of programming for the network. Losing the show would mean, in the view of CBC management, having to create the same amount of original programming. According to Stursberg, a one-hour drama show costs between $400,000 and $450,000 to make and the best it can draw in advertising revenue is $200,000. While not all of those 400 hours would be filled with original drama programs, that is still a hefty loss by Stursberg's reckoning.

Without hockey, there would be no way the CBC could pay for even a fraction of that programming. Stursberg figured that would mean the CBC would be forced into endless repeats of other shows and its already plunging viewership would crater. "It would be the greatest calamity in CBC's history and I would be blamed," he wrote.

Seven years later, Orridge and McEneaney were also keenly aware of the importance of keeping the NHL contract. "It would cost the network a significant amount of resources to acquire replacement programming for the content we're still able to broadcast on *Hockey Night*. It's over 300 hours of prime-time programming. To understand on Saturday night you would still be competing against hockey in Canada [with replacement programming], the numbers would probably pale in comparison," Orridge told *The Globe and Mail* in explaining why the CBC took the deal Rogers offered in the wake of winning the NHL contract.

A rival network executive was not so sure. He figured the CBC could run movies on Saturday nights and still make some money, which is more than it's making on the Rogers deal. The corporation could also do things like "extend Rick Mercer for another six weeks. That's not going to cost millions of dollars," the executive said.

Lacroix agreed that the "hundreds of hours of programming" that would need to be replaced would not all need to be original shows. He said there were a lot of options, including movies and news, but in the end anything the CBC put up would have to go against hockey on Saturday night, which meant negligible ratings. Lacroix pointed out, "If you look at what other broadcasters have done on Saturday night you'll see they have used those slots as giveaway slots."

Scott Moore, who was familiar with the CBC's finances from his days as head of CBC Sports and the revenue department, did not see things as dire as Stursberg. But he still felt losing *Hockey Night* just wasn't an option for the CBC.

"We did an analysis of it when I was at CBC," Moore said. "It's not so much the cost of Saturday night. On Saturday night, you could put movies in or repeats. It's the two months of play-offs, every night in prime time during all the US networks' season finales. You can't do repeats. You have to put scripted program-ming in. The cost there could be as high as $50, 60 million to replace that. That's why the [Rogers] deal with the CBC actually makes a great deal of sense for them."

Either way, that is what was hanging over Orridge and McEneaney as they went into negotiations with Bettman and Collins. While it may explain why they later agreed to the Rogers deal after the battle was lost, it does not explain why they were not interested in potential partnerships with either Bell or Rogers. Nor does it explain why they also declined a proposal from Bettman and Collins that would have allowed the CBC to keep a scaled-down version of *Hockey Night* and still have a chance to make money from it.

When the serious negotiations started, Bettman and Collins laid out for McEneaney and Orridge just how they felt the CBC could remain part of a television package that was clearly beyond the network's means, one that would eventually be a tremen-dous leap in revenue for the NHL. Like Phil King, Bettman and Collins offered the CBC a scaled-down version of *Hockey Night in Canada*. The network would get two games per week, preserving the traditional Saturday night doubleheaders. There would no longer be regional broadcasts across the country featuring all seven Canadian teams. The CBC would also get the Toronto Maple Leafs as the first game on most nights, which practically guaranteed the CBC would be the most-watched network on Saturdays, as long as the Leafs could finally get their act together. Also in the mix for the early Saturday games were the Montreal Canadiens, who draw the second-highest TV audiences in Canada. But outside of the second game of the doubleheader, which would feature at least one Western Canadian team, the other games involving Canadian teams would be shown on other networks. Also, the

CBC had to surrender more playoff games to other rights-holders, along with the digital rights and the NHL All-Star Game. Bettman and Collins would also guarantee the CBC could carry the Stanley Cup final for at least a few years. We understand your financial situation, the CBC people were told, and this will cost you more money than the previous contract but we're willing to work out a number. Bettman and Collins did not say exactly how much they were looking for in the package but most of the industry experts figured it would have cost the CBC around $200 million per year, almost double the previous contract. It was a big number, to be sure, but one a lot of observers figured the network could manage.

"Yeah, this is our model and this is what we're asking," Collins said in summing up how the proposal was presented to Orridge and McEneaney. But, just like the aftermath of the governors' meeting in Ottawa in 2012, Collins said, there was "a little bit of a disconnect."

Despite the rough ride he received on the air over the years, and the sense that CBC's upper management did not value the NHL properly, Bettman felt strongly that the CBC should remain in the picture. The way Bettman and Collins saw it, their plan allowed the CBC to maintain its grip on a show that became a cultural institution after more than 60 years on the air. And in practical terms, profits from *Hockey Night in Canada* provided funding for many other CBC programs. Keeping the show in-house with the CBC still generating revenue from it might also save some of the hundreds of jobs the network planned on cutting in the next few years. But to do so, the CBC people would have to be willing to work with other rights-holders, particularly when it came to broadcasting Saturday games and the playoffs.

"We were also trying to let them know they would have to partner with somebody," Collins said. "We liked our model, we thought it was a much better model. We ideally wanted to keep *Hockey Night* on CBC, which ultimately Rogers did."

Unfortunately, Orridge and McEneaney did not take up the offer. They eventually came back with a formal offer that essentially maintained the form of the expiring contract. The attitude was that if a Canadian team is playing on Saturday night, it will be on the CBC. There was a dollar amount the CBC was willing to pay for the rights but no one from the network has ever said on the record what it was. Two different media reports made a stab at it, with one citing sources as saying it was $175 million per year over 10 years and the other pegging it at $200 million. A few days after the Rogers deal was announced, the *Toronto Star* ran a story saying its sources said the CBC offered around $150 million annually on a deal that ranged from 7 to 10 years with the NHL demanding $200 million.

To say Bettman and Collins were disappointed by the response was putting it mildly. And it was deep disappointment rather than anger, because they felt the network bosses were not being realistic. Their attitude seemed to be that we've been a great partner all these years and we've done a great job. But we can't afford what you're looking for, although you should take it anyway. There was no sense they were aware Bell and Rogers were both waiting in the wings with their enormous chequebooks.

"It was a little bit naïve," Collins said. "That was kind of it and kind of an assumption that it would work out, that there weren't these sharks [Bell and Rogers]."

As for the offer, Collins said, "the CBC came back with a bit of the status quo. It was more like we appreciate what you guys laid out but this is all we can pay you. We don't get carriage fees, we can only generate this much in advertising, we don't have other avenues to exploit, we're at a disadvantage to wireless and cable companies. So we can do this much for you but you get the platform of CBC, you get to use *Hockey Night*, you get all the great traditional benefits of the institution.

"It was thought [by the CBC executives] that that would carry the day. To Gary's credit, [when] we left there, they had some term left in the exclusive negotiating window. We said it's a problem because it's nowhere near the kind of money we're looking for. But we'll try to be creative in terms of trying to give you what you need. It's not going to be what you want, but to see how we might create some value in other areas that might ultimately bridge it. That was in the good spirit of partnership that we left it. As we came closer to the end of the term, we'd come back together and try to see if there was a way to get a deal done."

Orridge insisted in a 2014 interview with *The Globe and Mail* that the offer he and McEneaney made was realistic even if it was, admittedly, based on the old model.

"We're not a vertically-integrated media company so we don't have the myriad of assets that a Rogers has," he said. "We can only monetize it over a much more narrow set of platforms than Rogers can. So it necessarily inhibited us from making an even more financially substantial offer because our offer still had to make sense.

"That's one of the inhibiting factors, just the way we're designed. So we could not compete with a Rogers for something like that. I think we extracted the best possible scenario going forward where once again Canadians can still see the high quality, the gold-medal standard in hockey production on CBC on Saturday nights."

When he was asked directly if Bettman and Collins had offered a scaled-down version of *Hockey Night*, Orridge at first dodged the question. He went on at length about how *Hockey Night* would still be on the CBC: "You know, arguably the institution is preserved for at least another four years and there is potential for it going beyond four years with the relationship with Rogers."

Later, when he was pressed whether or not Bettman and Collins made the offer, Orridge said, "I don't think that's an accurate characterization. I can't disclose, certainly, the negotiations, the content of the negotiations. But I can say we were very aggressive with our offer. We were very intent on keeping *Hockey Night in Canada* on CBC as it had been for 62 years. We were doing everything we could to preserve that type of relationship and that type of content offering."

Lacroix insisted the CBC accepted the fact it would not get as many Saturday and playoff games in the new deal and went so far as to discuss the numbers with Bettman and Collins. "We were all okay with this and we continued negotiating to the end because we were realistic with our dollars and we had to get as much as we could for the dollars we could put on the table," Lacroix said.

For their part, Orridge argued that he and McEneaney were well aware of the danger posed by Bell and Rogers and in the end they could not have done anything about it.

"No matter what we put on the table it would not have eclipsed the 5.2 billion dollars Rogers offered," Orridge said. "I think suffice it to say we did everything conceivable and we went through every conceivable scenario, we used strategic approaches, analytic approaches, common-sense approaches, we ran the numbers, we ran the research, we did everything we possibly could to come up with an offer that was significant, aggressive yet responsible."

To the CBC's point that the network did not have the revenue streams that Bell or Rogers had, both Collins and Scott Moore were sympathetic. They knew it was practically impossible to make a billion-dollar offer when your only method of recouping that money is to raise the advertising rates. Once the NHL set its sights on the gatekeeper model, which appears to have happened not long after the CBC's exclusive negotiating period, the CBC was out for good as the main rights-holder. Bell and Rogers could both sell wireless, mobile, cable and network subscriptions to raise revenue, none of which were available to the CBC.

"The key to the gatekeeper model is the subscription fees," Moore said. "Unless you had a Sportsnet that you were pretty sure you could increase subscription fees on, it wouldn't work. CBC would have had to take the risk of [paying] the 5.2 billion and hope to lay off the rights on Sportsnet."

After the approaches by Rogers and Bell to the CBC came up in conversations with Pelley and other sources for this book, an interview request was made to Orridge. He responded with an angry reference to a story I wrote for *The Globe and Mail* in October 2014 about how he and McEneaney did not accept the proposal Bettman and Collins made for a scaled-down version of *Hockey Night in Canada*. He argued the sub-licence deal he eventually made with Rogers saved jobs at CBC Sports. I replied with a list of topics I wanted to discuss, including the sub-licensing discussions with Bell and Rogers. Orridge did not respond.

While Collins fully understood the CBC's financial problems, he did not understand why the network was so resistant when it came to taking on either Bell or Rogers as a partner. Both he and Bettman felt it would have been nice to keep the CBC as a partner rather than simply a carrier of the broadcasts but there were things other than money that played a role in the split as well.

"It seemed to be a perfect storm happening at the CBC at that time," Collins said. "They were under enormous financial pressure, they were having cutbacks and programming changes all over the place. They didn't have a lot of money. They didn't have a lot to play with. They were kind of on their own there. The lack of interest in reaching out for a saviour, and making [the offer] their own deal ultimately hurt. Again, the guys who were running the show at that point had been good partners and stewards of the moment of a relationship that was incredibly successful. But it was time for a new model."

Lacroix said a dialogue continued with the NHL, even after the exclusive window closed and the CBC's offer was neither officially accepted nor rejected. But by then Bettman and Collins were looking past the public network, with the CBC's chances now reduced to being a junior partner to the eventual rights winner. It was the insistence of trying to keep all of the Canadian teams' games on Saturday night while still employing blackouts that really puzzled the NHL bosses.

"You could not argue that on the busiest night of hockey in the most passionate market in the world that you could have two games," said Collins, who may be an American but is fully aware of hockey's place in Canada. "You could have Toronto playing anyone, that would be the marquee game and would lead CBC even though there might be another great Canadian game in that window. Or there could be an amazing game elsewhere in the league, that could feature two Canadian heroes who played for American teams, and that would be blacked out. Nobody could see it.

"It didn't make a lot of sense not to give the fans what they want. Give fans the choice of what they want to watch. And aggregate the ratings. At the end of the day the assumption was you'd get more people watching hockey or watching longer if they had some choice.

"There were some great stories of what was happening throughut the league. Obviously we had spent a lot of time listening to CBC sort of whine when the Leafs didn't make the playoffs and playoff ratings were down. We said you're feeding that kind of behaviour because all you do is profile the Leafs, whether they're having a great year or not. Then you go from there to tell the story of the six Canadian clubs, which I get, but you're the national rights-holder.

"Then you maybe get into a handful of the best stories from around the league. I said there are great stories happening around the league every night, some about Canadians but not all. But this is the most passionate hockey market in the world, give them great hockey stories. You can lead with great Canadian stories because that's who you are."

5

THE BIG MONEY STEPS IN

While Collins and Bettman had firm ideas about how NHL games should be presented in the media, they still had a long way to travel before they found a receptive audience for their ideas about the broadcasts. Next up on the negotiating schedule was Bell Media. The conversation started with the multi-network, multi-night scenario. Hanging over the talks, which dragged through October, were a couple of shadows on the relationship between the NHL and Bell.

One was a feeling that the Bell executives were just a little too confident they had the contract in the bag. While Collins liked CTV president Phil King and Bell Media president Kevin Crull, he sensed they were not on the same page when it came to exactly how much the new contract would be worth, at least not in the early stages of the talks. The attitude seemed to be we will tell you how much we are willing to pay. Collins got the feeling that the Bell folks figured since the CBC could not pay a lot of money and Rogers was only interested in a Sunday-night package, there would not be a frenzied bidding war for the various network deals.

At this point, the gatekeeper model had not been discussed. Now Collins and Bettman had two of the three potential bidders make it clear they were not willing to make huge bids.

"Once we were out of the CBC window we were saying the same thing [to Bell]," Collins said. "We had a vision for Sunday night, we had a vision for what we wanted to do on Saturday, had a vision for how to distribute content generally on broadcast as well as digital. And we had two concepts, concepts where we'd kind of slice packages and get guys to bid on the individual packages, à la the NFL. We had a Saturday package, a Sunday night package, a Monday night package. As we got deeper into the conversations, we weren't going to get the kind of value we wanted. In a classic Canadian market sense, [the networks] were just going to cooperate as opposed to bidding against each other."

The other problem was potentially much bigger and it was similar to what was encountered with the CBC, only worse. This was the relationship between Gary Bettman and Bell Canada CEO George Cope. A contentious meeting between Bettman and Cope earlier in 2013 put a dent in their relationship, one that foreshadowed the negotiations later in the year for the NHL rights. The meeting concerned the French-language national NHL rights and the Montreal Canadiens' regional French rights for 60 games. The contracts were held by Bell's RDS network and had been for decades.

But now there was a new player on the scene with money and a mighty hankering to get in on the action: Québecor and its new TVA Sports network. Based in Montreal, Québecor is a media company like Bell and Rogers, with holdings in cable television, telecommunications, newspapers and broadcasting. This was the first time RDS faced any competition for the French rights of either the NHL or the Montreal Canadiens. Naturally Bettman and Collins wanted to capitalize on the highest bidder and things started off in early 2013 with exclusive talks with RDS as the existing rights-holder. However, the RDS and Bell officials made it clear they were only willing to pay so much, something else that foreshadowed the talks for the English deal that were several months away.

With Bell and RDS unwilling to budge on what they thought was a good price, the NHL was ready to postpone the talks until after the English deal was done in the fall of 2013. In an attempt to get the French talks back on track, a final meeting was proposed that would include Cope and Bettman.

The meeting did not go well. Cope has the public image of a bland, faceless business executive, probably because he doesn't give very many media interviews. But people who have done business with him can tell you the former varsity basketball player, who grew up in Port Perry, Ontario, just north of Toronto, plays to win and plays hard. Cope was not happy that Québecor and TVA Sports were now on the scene. He was not fond of Québecor because it was a competitor of Bell's. He apparently was also irked that TVA was given a chance to bid on the Canadiens' regional rights because Bell Canada owns 18 per cent of the team. The idea was that the Habs' rights should stay with an owner's network. Even though Bell owned a share of the Maple Leafs as well, the NHL allowed the double investment because Bell shuffled part of its MLSE purchase to its pension-plan arm, which technically meant Bell was a 28-per-cent owner of the Leafs, not 37.5. NHL rules say no one can own more than 30 per cent of one team while owning shares in another.

According to someone who was in the room, at one point the 6-foot-8 Cope, who towers over most people let alone Bettman, who might hit 5-foot-9 with his skates on, told the commissioner that in other parts of Bell Canada's business they do not work with people who choose to work with their competitors. Bettman was not pleased, the source said, especially since this was not the first time he and Cope crossed swords.

Some months earlier, during the NHL lockout, Cope was said to have given Bettman another earful in his guise as a member of the MLSE board of directors. Since the Toronto Maple Leafs is the wealthiest team in the NHL, MLSE was not happy with either of the last two lockouts, which saw millions in revenue disappear. The way Cope saw it, according to a source who knows him, is that Bettman might be the commissioner of the NHL but he is still an employee of the 30 team owners. Cope saw no need for any deference to the commissioner and saw no need to get to know Bettman and build a relationship after he became a team owner.

The funny thing is, there is a pecking order among professional sports owners even if they are all wealthy, successful businessmen. At the top are the people who own their teams outright, with their own money invested. In the NHL, that means men like Jeremy Jacobs, the Boston Bruins owner who is the chairman of the board of governors and the most powerful owner in the league. Or Murray Edwards, the majority owner of the Calgary Flames, or Geoff Molson of the Montreal Canadiens. They have skin in the game, as owners like to say. The CEOs who represent corporations that own teams do not have the same status. Cope may be a powerful figure in his own right but he is an employee of Bell Canada rather than an owner, so in the eyes of men like Jacobs and Bettman that is a bit different.

A request for Cope to discuss the incidents was placed with a Bell spokesman, who replied there would be no comment.

Again, the two run-ins were not enough by themselves to scuttle Bell's chances of cutting a deal with the NHL. But combined with Cope's decision not to get involved in the negotiations, just like Lacroix's absence from the talks, they were far from helpful. Bettman may give up some inches and pounds to Cope but he is not someone who can be intimidated. He also has a long memory.

Bell might have been able to counter the perceptions of Bettman and Collins if someone with a long and productive relationship with the NHL commissioner had been added to the negotiating team. That someone was former CTV and TSN president Rick Brace, who had negotiated several rights deals with Bettman in previous years and was said to have a warm relationship with him. But by 2013, Brace had been shuffled off to president of Bell Media's specialty networks and was not part of the negotiations.

However, the talks with Bell picked up when they moved from the multi-network, multi-night approach to the gatekeeper model. Bettman and Collins made a presentation of the model to King and Crull. They laid out how they saw it working, with one company buying all of the rights—television, radio, digital, wireless, streaming, even platforms that had not been invented yet—and then distributing the content. It would be up to the rights-holder to figure out how to monetize the package when it came to the newer platforms that appealed to millennials, like YouTube highlights.

This may have been where some of that assuredness on the part of King and Crull came into play. Bell Media had the infrastructure to handle the gatekeeper model. Rogers could compete on the digital and wireless fronts as well as with Sportsnet but it did not have anything comparable to the other over-the-air network, CTV. Indeed, Rogers Media president Keith Pelley figured Bettman and Collins drew up the gatekeeper model with Bell in mind.

"The gatekeeper model was all about Bell," Pelley said. "[The NHL] hadn't even considered Rogers at that point. I think everyone believed, and Bell believed, they were the only ones who could do it. They had CTV, with the biggest distribution, and TSN. We had City and Sportsnet. There's no question their distribution platforms, especially from a conventional perspective, were significantly higher than ours."

However, when Bettman, Collins and deputy commissioner Bill Daly met with Pelley and Moore for the first time, which was during the same period they were talking to Bell, the gatekeeper model did come up. It was almost as an afterthought. Bettman, Collins and Daly came to Rogers' headquarters in downtown Toronto in early September 2013. They met with Pelley and Moore in a Sportsnet boardroom to explore their interest in the NHL rights.

"We were in an internal conversation about what we're going to do, re the NHL rights," Pelley said. "I had heard wind that there was a gatekeeper model. So I asked the question midway through the meeting, what would happen if we wanted to buy all of it? Gary said is that something you would be interested in? I said, 'Yes, we're aggressive, we're ambitious and we're firmly entrenched in position number-two now but we want to be the dominant sports organization and you have the best property.'

"At that point Gary shut his book and said, 'Let's have that discussion. Why don't we come back tomorrow?' I said perfect. We came back the very next day. They did the entire proposal—I imagine they took the Bell logo off the book and put Rogers on it. At that particular time that's when I went okay, all right, game on!"

While Pelley was convinced the gatekeeper was the way to go for Rogers, Moore was not so sure. He thought the billions of dollars it would cost made the deal risky and he wasn't sure those at the top of Rogers management would go for it. "I remember Scott coming into my office afterwards," Pelley said. "He says, 'You don't think we could make this happen, do you?' I said why not, let's try it, let's take it all the way. Let's be bold!"

Pelley and Moore told the NHL group they would need time to prepare a bid. Bettman and Collins then turned their attention back to Bell while Pelley and Moore quietly started the groundwork. Before they could put together a pitch they had to secure the approval of Rogers CEO Nadir Mohamed, the board of directors and, most of all, Edward Rogers. That would take some time.

When it came to Bell Media, Collins felt King and Crull were more enthusiastic about the gatekeeper model than the other option.

"The Bell guys really embraced it," Collins said. "Phil King in particular, really was a champion for us inside that building. It changed the whole discussion because I think people really saw the possibilities. All of a sudden we had people being creative, really smart people who knew the business really well or were incredibly successful, had assets to deploy in promoting the game and monetizing the game. Now they were going to work around how to help us build that plan. Obviously [that was] to help them make money but it was clear the league was going to make a lot more money going down this road."

King was excited about the idea of owning all of the NHL's media rights but sources close to Bell Media say it was more to do with having control rather than having all sorts of television programming at his disposal. While King and Crull were certainly interested in buying the gatekeeper model and willing to pay a lot of money for it, they were not planning to go it alone.

"[Bell] had no intention of trying to keep all of it like Rogers," a source familiar with Bell Media's plans said. "It was too much money. [Bell] would have to offset some of this."

The way King and Crull saw things, it would be too difficult to sell that many games, a full schedule of as many as three nights a week of hockey. Trying to sell advertising on that many games "would be a crazy idea," according to one insider.

Again, King and Crull figured if they got the Canadian national deal, they would not renew any of the team's regional rights once they expired. The CBC also came back in the picture with the gatekeeper model on roughly the same terms King laid out to Orridge in the multi-network scenario. King told Orridge the CBC still wasn't out of the running, that all he had to do was sit tight and not take sides with either Bell or Rogers and someone would take care of them.

"No doubt [the CBC] would have paid a lot more for less but everybody was paying a lot more for less," said a source familiar with Bell's plans. "There's no other network that can blow out the month of April, prime time every night. CTV can't do it, City can't do it, even TSN and [Sportsnet] have a hard time doing it because of Raptors, Jays, and all the other stuff. So [they] will need a partner."

Just when King told Orridge to sit tight is not clear but it may have been just before Bell and the NHL moved on to discussing the gatekeeper model. Lacroix said Bettman decreed that none of the bidders could talk to each other, apparently after the CBC's window closed. "Yes, it was to our advantage to sit on the sidelines because we thought we would be a good partner to both [Bell or Rogers]," Lacroix said.

In hindsight, it is easy to say King and Crull underestimated the threat from Rogers. But at the time, aside from the messages put out by Pelley and Moore about maybe not bidding, the Bell folks saw no reason to think Rogers would chase the gatekeeper model. "Why would they do this? It's insane," one of the Bell executives said about Rogers. "They have all the regional games, they have the Jays, they're tiny, they don't have CTV, they don't have the French component. That seemed logical."

At the time, Rogers had the regional rights to the Vancouver Canucks, Calgary Flames, Edmonton Oilers, the Maple Leafs and Ottawa Senators. All Bell had were the Winnipeg Jets and the Montreal Canadiens' English and French rights. The Rogers rights represented more than 200 regular-season games at a better price than the national rights. Sure, it did not include any playoff games but that meant Sportsnet didn't have to worry about fitting them into the Blue Jays' schedule in the spring.

By mid-November, following a presentation by King and Crull to the NHL television people, Bettman and Collins had an offer in hand from Bell for the rights. It was the gatekeeper model and it tied up the conventional television, radio, digital and wireless platforms plus any platform that had not yet been invented.

Included in the offer were some firm demands in exchange for the large amount of money Bell planned to fork over, chiefly concerning playoff scheduling. For years, Bettman had always given the US networks preferential treatment when it came to scheduling playoff games. That's why Canadian teams often saw their games played on a Saturday or Sunday afternoon on a sunny spring day, which did not do wonders for the television ratings. King made it clear to Bettman and Collins that if Bell was to pay more than double what NBC was, there would be no Leafs playoff games, should such a thing ever come to pass, at one o'clock on a Saturday afternoon.

The offer was for 12 years and the NHL would receive a total of $5.2 billion from Bell Media. Sound familiar?

The NHL's executives seemed to be impressed. They gave King and Crull the impression they were in the driver's seat. Collins, too, thought things were going well for Bell: "They came back and made a very compelling offer and had a really compelling vision for how they would program it out and how they would handle those rights. They came to the table loaded for bear."

Cope signed off on the $5.2-billion offer but that does not mean he was comfortable with it. Nor were King and Crull, although they thought it was necessary to ensure they landed the contract. The thinking was the deal had a 50-50 chance of making money by the end of the 12 years.

However, there was at least something of a shadow of a doubt hanging over the Bell offer. Several times during the negotiations, stretching back to the multi-network talks, Collins remarked to

King that Bell was treating this like just another media deal rather than a new style of partnership. This is a wireless deal, an Internet deal, a satellite deal, Collins said. "You're not wrapping your arms around the whole thing," was the way Collins put it to King, according to one source.

In the wake of the offer, as the word spread among the NHL's second tier of executives, King, Crull and other Bell executives like Gerry Frappier, president of RDS and French-language TV, and TSN president Stew Johnston heard from their various NHL counterparts that it looked like a lock. King asked Collins when they could expect a response and he was told a week or so.

But first Bettman and Collins had to hear from Rogers. They set a date one week later at the NHL offices in New York. Pelley and Moore had worked hard to get the people above them onside. As far as the pitch goes, they were well aware that Bettman was looking for someone to say they wanted to make the NHL players the story, not the broadcasters.

Both Moore and Pelley say they were also counting on a quick presentation to the NHL followed by a quick decision. That was why they avoided making a pitch on the same day as Bell and why they didn't want to go first. They did not want to make it easy for Bettman and Collins to get an auction sale going. "If we'd done it on the same day the outcome might have been very different," Moore said.

Drawing on his knowledge of Bettman from his days running CBC Sports, Moore insisted from the start that Rogers CEO Nadir Mohamed had to be a major part of the selling job.

"I can remember Nadir saying to Keith and I, 'Okay, you guys go get this deal,'" Moore said. "I said to Nadir you have to come. He said I've already announced my retirement. I said you have to come. I know Gary, he wants to be across the table from the most important guy in the company.

"That would be probably my biggest contribution. I had a longer history with Gary than Keith had. Because of the deal with the CBC I worked with him a lot. That made all the difference."

It only made a difference because Mohamed agreed to participate. A lot of CEOs in his position would not have done the same. He was due to step down in a couple of months and a successor, Guy Laurence, had already been named. No one would have blamed Mohamed if he just coasted through his remaining weeks.

But Mohamed wasn't the only one who needed convincing. Most important of all, Pelley had to sell Edward Rogers on the idea. If the family did not buy in, this deal would simply not get done. There was also the Rogers board of directors and its cast of family loyalists headed by chairman Alan Horn. This was a tall order and it was left to Pelley with support from Moore. Pelley is an excitable fellow with infectious enthusiasm and although it was not all smooth sailing—a pitch to Laurence to get on board was met with something close to indifference—he managed to get the support he needed.

"I was really, really, really bullish on this," Pelley said. "I believed that it was the most coveted content and to be able to acquire it for 12 years across multiple platforms was something that was a game-changer for us and Rogers.

"The length of the contract and the magnitude of the contract was the super floss of the deal. Rallying the chairman Alan Horn and Edward and Nadir, it was quite phenomenal to do that and I give Scott Moore a ton of credit. It was Scott and I that were trumpeting this. Once we got the okay to do it, making that call to John Collins and Gary and saying, 'Gary, we're ready to have a serious conversation,' I thought was pretty exciting."

The other important job Pelley had was signing up a French partner. The obvious and only choice was Québecor's TVA Sports. The network was only a couple of years old by then but was aggressively looking for programming in order to catch up to Bell

Media's RDS. Rogers already had an agreement with TVA to provide production resources. Pelley laid out his plans to Pierre Dion, president and CEO of Québecor's TVA Group Inc., and found a receptive audience. Dion's decision to pay more than $100 million to annually sub-license the national French rights and to battle RDS for the Montreal Canadiens' French regional rights, which were also up for auction at the time, gave Rogers the financial cushion it needed to land the contract, according to both Pelley and Collins.

"From my point of view, Rogers never gets there without Pierre," Collins said. "His willingness to spend on the French national rights and the gap between what he was willing to spend and what Bell, RDS, was willing to spend, is what really made the deal for Rogers."

Serendipity struck as well, since the Wednesday they would meet with Bettman and Collins fell during Grey Cup week. That meant all of the Bell Media executives would be preoccupied with the CFL festivities in Regina and in poor position to drop everything to rescue their bid if that became necessary. Or, as one broadcaster would say later, "we were all in Regina freezing our asses as we're getting fucked."

The Rogers team's plan was to make a three-part presentation and follow it up by asking for a quick and firm decision from Bettman. Another gamble was that it would be made plain to the NHL that if there was no decision on the contract that day, Rogers would pull its bid permanently. The Rogers people had an idea of what kind of money the NHL was looking for but not the exact amount.

Mohamed was to open the presentation with a speech about how committed Rogers was to the NHL. Then Moore and Pelley would outline what they had in mind for the broadcasts and the other coverage of the league, with an emphasis on the deal being a partnership rather than Rogers acting just as a rights-holder. The final part of the presentation was how much Rogers was prepared to pay for all of this.

The party flew down to New York on the Rogers corporate jet on the day of the meeting. Aside from Mohamed, Pelley and Moore, there were Rogers chief financial officer Tony Staffieri and company lawyer Mike Webber. Also along for the ride were two Rogers researchers, who would be stationed along with their computers in a McDonald's across the street from the NHL offices to provide any statistics or other detailed information needed by the team.

"When we took off, Tony turned to me and said, 'What do you think is going to happen today?' " Moore remembered. "I said, 'We're going to have a deal. As long as we're still in the room, as long as they don't throw us out we have a chance of making a deal.' "

Mohamed was the opening act and Moore said he played his role to the hilt. "What Nadir said beautifully, his opening speech was all about the commitment of the family, the commitment of the family to sports, Ted [Rogers] having bought the Blue Jays. It was an amazing opening remark. He was brilliant," Moore said.

Next up was Moore, who knew what Bettman wanted to hear. He also knew that Bell's presentation was made more along the lines of a traditional media deal in that they will give you all this money and in return they expect this, this and this, such as preference on playoff dates.

"It was about promoting the stars of the game," Moore said. "We talked about, it was Keith's idea, the Olympic model, of going and talking about and doing long profiles on some key stars of the game.

"I think it's the difference between being a long-term partner and taking them for granted and somebody coming in and wanting to do things differently. Keith's mantra from the beginning was let's make this a partnership. So there was the partnership thing, the building the stars thing, and the very important thing was we brought Nadir to the table. Gigantic."

The group also made it clear the entire Rogers corporation would be involved in promoting the NHL. The league's logo would be on the company's well-known red vans and trucks, for example. And on the cable bills sent to customers. Non-sports outlets owned by Rogers would start paying attention to the league and its teams.

While Mohamed, Moore and Pelley were charming Bettman, Collins and probably Daly, it was left to Rogers CFO Staffieri to gauge how the pitch was going over. "We said, 'Okay, we made our presentation, we'd like to take 10 minutes and come back with the financials,' " Moore said. "They left the room, we turned to Tony and said what's your reading? He said you've got the deal. As soon as we said we want to work with you to grow the game and build stars, Tony said Gary's eyes lit up. We knew that wasn't the tone of what the other guys had done. We were also the last guys to make the presentation."

What happened next proved Staffieri to be right. In part three of the presentation, Bettman and Collins were shown what Rogers was willing to pay. But it was not as much as Bell's $5.2 million. After some numbers were tossed back and forth, Pelley and Moore told Mohamed it would be a good idea to go into Bettman's office for a one-on-one chat with the commissioner. After the conference, during which it is thought Mohamed told Bettman if they could not come to an agreement the Rogers bid was off the table, Mohamed came back out and spoke to his team.

"I believe what Nadir told us," Moore said. "Gary said to him we like your presentation, we think you'll be great partners, here's what I need. It will be basically a dollar more than what's on the table. If you can get to that, you've got a deal."

It was a stretch, so they had to go back to Edward Rogers for his approval on the final bump in price, which was actually

$1 million more than Bell's $5.2 billion. Pelley also had to see if Dion was willing to raise Québecor's stake in the deal to $125 million per year. Both men said yes and Mohamed told Bettman they would raise their offer as long as there was a quick decision. They had a deal.

In the end, Bettman made the decision to anoint Rogers as the NHL's national broadcaster for 12 years by himself. There is no doubt he was heavily influenced by Mohamed's enthusiastic presence in the negotiations. A source close to Bettman was asked how important this was. "Very," was the reply. Also playing into it was Bettman's relationship with Moore and Pelley over the years.

"While the Bell guys were obviously well respected, I think the Rogers guys were well loved," Collins said. "And that probably made the difference. But that difference was Gary's. Gary made the call."

On the question of how much Cope's adversarial relationship with Bettman played into the decision, it is hard to say. But it is notable that Bettman did not give Bell, its existing partner, the final word on the Rogers offer.

In a sense, the Rogers group was stunned. They managed to pull off a $5.2-billion transaction in a matter of days. All of their gambles, from staying out of the negotiations until the end so they could avoid making their pitch on the same day as Bell to bringing Mohamed to the table, paid off. They walked in the door of the NHL offices at 10:00 that morning and had the agreement by 4 p.m. The plan was to announce the deal publicly the following Tuesday.

"It was amazing how quickly it came together and it was amazing how the element of surprise was the true winner," Pelley said. "We made a decision to go for it, we went down to see John Collins and Gary and within 72 hours we shook hands."

Pelley's 72-hour reference was to the final handshake with Bettman and Collins that came on the following Sunday, November

24, Grey Cup Sunday. That came after a frenzied weekend of work on the details of the deal involving Rogers, the CBC and the NHL. On Sunday, Rogers and the NHL banged out a short memorandum of understanding, which was the only part of the contract on paper.

Once Bettman made a verbal commitment to Rogers followed by handshakes and at least one hug (Moore said it was the first time he ever hugged Bettman) on Wednesday, the clock started ticking on those contract details. If a press conference were to be held by the next Tuesday a lot of work needed to get done quickly. The first and biggest task was to cut a sub-licensing deal with the CBC for *Hockey Night in Canada*. Hubert Lacroix, Neil McEneaney and Jeffrey Orridge didn't know it yet but they were about to enter a shotgun marriage with Rogers that had to be consummated within 72 hours so the last details with the NHL contract could be nailed down.

Meanwhile, in Regina, a small football-mad city that was the antithesis to the Big Apple where billions of dollars were changing hands in another sport, a lot of TSN people were confidently telling others it looked like they were going to wind up keeping the NHL to go along with their football package. But some Bell Media people were feeling out of sorts with the Grey Cup party atmosphere around them. They were getting antsy. They had heard nothing from Bettman and Collins after making their offer. An increasingly impatient Cope asked Phil King several times what was going on. So around the same time Pelley and company were making their pitch to the NHL, King stepped away from the Grey Cup noise to place a call to Collins in New York.

Collins told King that his offer was looking good but there were a lot of details to sort out. He said it would take a few more days. King went back to Cope and the other Bell Media executives and said the deal was not a slam dunk but he thought they were still in good shape and would hear something the following week.

The confidence of some TSN executives was reflected in the media because items started to appear, saying it looked like both TSN and CBC would hang on to their shares of the NHL rights. But back in Toronto and New York there was a frenzy of activity.

The morning after the jubilant Rogers executives flew home Wednesday night on the company jet, Bettman got on the phone. He called CBC president Hubert Lacroix and said he wanted to speak to him and his negotiating team on a conference call that afternoon. Neither Lacroix nor Orridge nor McEneaney knew what Bettman was going to say. But there was at least some hope it might be good news about the offer they submitted back in August. Bettman did say he might get back to them.

Wrong. Bettman told the three executives he decided to sell all of the rights to one company. He didn't say which one but ended the call by saying they would hear from Keith Pelley. It was clear all three CBC executives were stunned by the call.

Pelley called in a few minutes to set up a meeting with McEneaney and Orridge. Lacroix remained in Montreal, where he lives. Within an hour, they met at the Intercontinental Hotel in downtown Toronto, just up the street from CBC's Front Street headquarters. Pelley and Scott Moore were there along with Jack Tomik, Rogers' senior vice-president of media sales. Tomik knew both McEneaney and Orridge well because until he went to Rogers a year earlier he was CBC's head of revenue, having replaced Moore in that position when the latter went to Rogers. Like the NHL players who were the targets of this pursuit, Canadian broadcast executives tend to move from team to team.

Tomik conducted the first meeting on behalf of Rogers. He sat down with McEneaney, Orridge and Jacques Gaboury, CBC's legal counsel. The CBC executives were told what was going to happen next, as Tomik was well aware they desperately wanted to keep a share of the NHL rights. He was fresh from the CBC so he as well as Moore knew it would cost around $60 million to produce enough original programming to replace *Hockey Night*. Tomik also pointed out that even after the CBC spent that $60 million, it would not get good ratings for the programming because it would have to go up against *Hockey Night*, so they wouldn't get any revenue from it. Oh, and by the way, you have less than a year to get this scripted programming up and running, which is pretty much impossible.

Next up in the one-two punch were Pelley and Moore. They went in and laid out the sub-licensing deal they had in mind for *Hockey Night in Canada*. Pelley did most of the talking. He set aside his usual gregarious manner and came on strong. He told the CBC group the deal was not up for negotiation and he required an answer in 48 hours. The CBC would get to keep *Hockey Night* and its Saturday night doubleheaders. But the show would now be controlled by Rogers, along with the advertising revenue. Rogers would take all of the advertising inventory and revenue. Nothing would go to the CBC but there would be some room for the network to promote its other shows. The CBC would also pay Rogers a certain amount for producing the show by paying cash plus providing the new owners with their technical staff (who would continue to be paid by the CBC). Pelley said Rogers needed studio and office space in the CBC building and it was to be provided rent-free. If any of these demands could not be met, the CBC would lose *Hockey Night*.

"No, they didn't see us coming at all," Pelley said of the CBC reaction to the news from Bettman that Rogers was the winner of the gatekeeper sale. Indeed, according to a Bell Media source, Orridge was expecting a call from them, not from Rogers, as both he and the Bell people thought their bid would carry the day. Instead it was Rogers, and what they were offering was nothing like the soft landing Bell Media had in mind for the public network.

The double shock—first losing an institution of 62 years that paid a lot of bills around the network and then given 48 hours to agree to a one-sided deal to keep the programming side of it—must have had the CBC executives reeling.

"If you look at it from their point of view for a second, they get a call from Gary. They didn't really know much about the gate-keeper. They thought they could keep *Hockey Night* pretty much on the terms they had it," Moore said. "Whether that's naïve or not … Then they get a call from Gary saying, 'Hey after 62 years you're out and you're going to get a visit from three men in dark suits from Rogers.' There was an emotional sort of shell shock to that."

Lacroix, however, disputed the notion Pelley presented his demands in such a hard-ball manner. "If you really think that was the conversation with Rogers … Rogers has more respect for CBC/Radio-Canada than that," he said. Lacroix said there were extensive negotiations that went on all weekend with the deal finally getting signed just before he went on stage Tuesday, November 26, 2013, with Pelley, Mohamed and Bettman to make the big announcement.

Rogers executives paint a different picture. They say that while talks did make for a hectic weekend beginning with the first encounter with the CBC people on Thursday, they were not so much haggling over the major take-it-or-leave-it terms presented by Pelley as filling in the details. This included putting a monetary value on the things Rogers wanted, like the CBC paying for the technical staff and how much studio and office space was needed and how much it was worth.

The Rogers team was split into three groups with Moore and Pelley spreading themselves among the groups. Moore and Jack Tomik handled the talks with the CBC people. Rogers CFO Tony Staffieri led the discussions with Québecor about the French national rights and Moore, Pelley and company legal officer Mike Webber dealt with the NHL. "I don't think any of us got much sleep that weekend. There was a war room set up with three different major agreements going on all at once," Moore said.

No one was sweating things more than Pelley. He may have come on strong with his demands to the CBC but he also knew he needed the public network as badly as the CBC needed to hang on to *Hockey Night in Canada*. Unlike Bell with CTV, Rogers did not have an over-the-air network that covered almost all of Canada. It had City, which was in several major cities and a couple of smaller communities but had no presence in Atlantic Canada. The CBC negotiators could have pushed back and told Pelley he wasn't going to get their airwaves for free, that they deserved a share of the advertising revenue or to buy the games outright and sell their own advertising.

Pelley fully expected that to be the reaction of Orridge and McEneaney. His only fallback plan was to approach Shaw Communications Inc., which at the time owned Global Television, Canada's third over-the-air network. But Global did not cover Canada nearly as much as the CBC did.

The talks between Rogers and the various groups involved went on every day from Thursday through Sunday and well into the evening. For example, the CBC and Rogers had to work out exactly what was involved with the public network providing its own production staff—the producers, directors and other behind-the-scenes people like camera operators and sound technicians—along with free office and studio space. They agreed on an annual dollar value for this, called cash-in-kind, and it was paired with actual cash, 50-50, as the amount the CBC would pay as part of the production cost. One protection for the CBC was that once that dollar value was reached, any further costs, which often meant overtime for the staff, would be paid by Rogers.

One odd thing was that neither Orridge nor McEneaney were a constant presence during the talks. According to a *Toronto Star* story that cited both men as sources, Orridge coached his son's basketball team in a tournament in the Toronto area through the weekend while McEneaney was in cottage country in Huntsville,

Ontario, with his son's hockey team. They stayed in touch with the CBC team by telephone. If the CBC were really negotiating the major terms of the sub-licensing deal rather than ironing out details, it stands to reason both executives would have been as involved in person as Pelley and Moore.

By Sunday morning, November 24, documents for the deal between the CBC and Rogers were exchanged but nothing was set in stone. Pelley flew to Montreal early Sunday evening to see Lacroix in person. The *Toronto Star* story said Lacroix met Pelley at Trudeau Airport and gave him a Christmas cookie in the shape of a snowman "to honour him for his efforts to fly to meet him." Pelley, according to a source with knowledge of the weekend's events, had a blunt message for Lacroix: that's the deal. You either want *Hockey Night* and the brand or you'll lose it. I'll go to Global if I have to. Pelley then got back on a plane and flew home. By late Sunday night, the CBC negotiating team agreed to Pelley's terms.

This came as not only a great relief to Pelley but a great surprise. He expected the CBC to come back, note how much Rogers needed its Canadian reach and reject a deal that called for it to not only provide office and studio space rent-free but to hand over paid staff plus cash for *Hockey Night in Canada* and get nothing in return. Zero advertising revenue. If Orridge and McEneaney had agreed to let Rogers keep all of the advertising inventory but in exchange would have to pay rent for the network's facilities and pay for the staff, Pelley likely would have agreed.

Once again, almost like the NHL deal, surprise and speed won the day. The CBC people were not expecting to hear from Rogers, they thought TSN would be the winner, and they were not given much time to make up their minds.

But Lacroix remained comfortable with the deal, even with the benefit of hindsight. He pointed out the NHL deal with Rogers is "exactly the same deal" the CBC has with Sportsnet and TSN for the Olympics, which started in 2014, but in reverse. The CBC keeps all the ad revenue with Rogers and Bell paying rights fees for the right to air some events. The CBC is the one taking the risk it can sell all of the advertising time. But that deal is only for about three weeks every two years when the Games are on and it is for a lot less money.

"Whoever is the one paying the rights is the one taking the risk and gets all the revenues and you get the content," Lacroix said in August 2017. "That was the beginning, interestingly enough, to how our Olympic deal got done. There were many advantages to CBC doing this in light of what happened. I still feel four or five years into it, with hindsight, that it was a pretty good deal."

The contract was signed by both sides and presented to CBC's board of directors on Monday afternoon. It was approved by the end of the day.

While the talks with the CBC were going on, Moore, Pelley and Rogers' legal vice-president Mike Webber were putting together something on paper with the NHL. This involved a visit to the New York NHL office by the Rogers people and they had a signed memorandum of understanding by Sunday. It was really just a short outline of the contract but it made Mohamed, Staffieri and Webber a lot more comfortable. Pelley and Moore weren't as nervous about not having a fully drawn-up and signed contract ahead of Tuesday's press conference.

"When we left [the NHL office the previous Wednesday] all we had was a handshake with Gary," Moore said. "There was no paper. Tony [Staffieri] and Nadir [Mohamed] and Mike Webber, they were all really, really concerned about the fact we didn't have anything on paper. I said, 'Whether you like Gary or not, if you have a handshake with him it's a done deal. Turned out, not only was it a done deal that day, we got it on paper on the Sunday."

If Moore and Pelley had known then what was going on behind the scenes with the NHL, they would have become as jittery as their Rogers colleagues. According to multiple sources, things were not entirely settled at the NHL head office after Bettman decided on the Wednesday afternoon to give Rogers the 12-year contract. Deputy commissioner Bill Daly and chief operating officer John Collins were not comfortable with the idea that Bell Media would not get a chance to top Rogers' offer. After all, Bell was the existing rights-holder and it was common practice in the sports world to give the incumbent that courtesy. Collins and Daly tried to persuade Bettman to do so. However, the commissioner felt so strongly he wanted Rogers as a new partner that he refused.

By this time, though, knowledge of what was going on with Rogers seeped beyond Bettman, Daly and Collins. Somehow, according to sources, someone got word to George Cope, perhaps via MLSE, that Mohamed, Pelley and Moore were down in New York scooping the broadcast deal out from under Bell Media. Cope was told if he wanted to save Bell's offer he should get on a plane for New York.

But Cope decided not to act. Since a Bell spokesman said he would not comment when an interview request was made, Cope's reasons are not clear. One source thinks Cope was already unhappy about risking $5.2 billion on the NHL rights and he had just spent $3.4 billion buying Astral Media, which owned 80 radio stations and numerous specialty television channels across Canada. Another source feels Cope did not really believe Rogers would go through with the deal, having some heavy financial commitments of its own, such as bumping the Blue Jays payroll by nearly $40 million per year, so that when it came time to write the cheque the company executives would falter. Whatever the reasoning, Cope's decision meant there was no obstacle—and who is to say Bettman would have listened to an 11th-hour pitch given his relationship with the Bell CEO? By Monday afternoon, Pelley, Moore, Bettman and company were ready to call for a Tuesday morning announcement at Rogers' headquarters at the corner of Bloor and Jarvis Streets in Toronto.

Naturally, the announcement was a stunner for the sports and broadcasting worlds. But more nervous days and nights were ahead for Pelley and Moore.

6

CELEBRATING THE CHANGE

Even though the broadcasting world, like the journalism and hockey worlds for that matter, is really a village where most of the inhabitants have worked at all of the major outlets at one time or another and know each other well, word about the unprecedented deal between Rogers and the NHL did not leak out immediately. Indeed, a few media reports that came out as Pelley and Moore were wrapping up the contract with Bettman and Collins indicated the NHL was headed towards another multi-network, multi-night format. There was no mention of a gatekeeper.

The first report actually came from a publication in the United States, the respected *Sports Business Journal*. This appeared on Monday, November 25, 2013, and stated the NHL and the CBC were finalizing a 10-year deal for *Hockey Night in Canada* that was part of a series of contracts with five networks. According to the story, the NHL would soon sign with the CBC, TSN, Sportsnet, RDS and TVA for a total of $350 million per year, a healthy bump from the $190 million it took in under its previous agreements with the CBC, TSN and RDS. TSN would gain additional playoff games and the NHL All-Star Game at the expense of the CBC, the story added, and it looked like Sportsnet would get a package of Sunday night games. The CBC was alleged to be forking over the most money among the networks at $175 million per year, with TSN and Sportsnet combining to pay $125 million and RDS and TVA paying a total of $50 million for the French-language rights.

This story fell in line with hints that had been appearing in the media in previous days, a lot of them seemingly based on conversations with the large group of TSN executives who were in Regina for Grey Cup week. By that point, with no official word from the NHL and the belief Rogers was not a serious threat, the TSN people still felt they had the upper hand.

But by Monday afternoon, word began to spread among NHL and broadcast insiders that Bell Media was out and Rogers was in. There were also whispers the CBC managed to hang on to *Hockey Night*, although it seemed everyone was under the impression it was in some form of the network's previous deal, not with a one-sided sub-licence agreement.

On Monday morning, the day after the Grey Cup, president of CTV and sports programming Phil King headed for the airport in Regina with a group of his fellow Bell Media executives, including TSN president Stew Johnston and Mark Milliere, TSN's senior vice-president of production. After his flight landed in Toronto, King was headed to the baggage claim when he fielded telephone calls from both Bob McKenzie and James Duthie, two of TSN's hockey broadcasters. They told King they were hearing TSN might be out. King had been reassuring colleagues for a few days, based on his conversation with John Collins and Bill Daly the previous week, that they should relax, more would be known in a day or two. He did so again with McKenzie and Duthie and went home. Several hours later, his phone rang again.

"Monday night about 10 p.m., I get a call from Kevin Crull," King said. "He says Phil I got some news for you. Sure, what's up?

We're out of the NHL. What? That's crazy. We're not out. No, I'm telling you, Bettman just called George [Cope] and said we're out. There's an announcement tomorrow."

TSN even got the scoop on the shocking development, thanks to McKenzie, the ultimate hockey insider. While King was still absorbing the shock delivered by Crull, McKenzie posted this on Twitter on Monday night: "Pains me to report this, but NHL closing in on landmark CDN TV deal with two CDN networks. Many years (10+), many billions. #overandout." A few hours later, early Tuesday morning, McKenzie had it nailed down: "Official announcement expected Tuesday by NHL: CBC and Rogers have exclusive English-language NHL rights deal. Believed to be 12 year deal."

Getting the scoop was cold comfort for McKenzie and everyone else at TSN. Besides, the Rogers broadcasters and reporters were undoubtedly told to clam up. Both Rogers and the NHL wanted to keep a lid on the big announcement until the press conference started on Tuesday at 11 a.m. in the theatre at Rogers' headquarters in Toronto.

While McKenzie was putting together his report about what came to be regarded as the sports story of the year in Canada, it appeared at least some CBC people still thought they had a chance to land a share of the NHL rights. Or they were trying to put their own spin on the one-sided deal with Rogers. A story in *The Globe and Mail* on Tuesday morning said the CBC was about to sign a new contract with the NHL to keep *Hockey Night in Canada* for as long as 10 years for $200 million a year, almost double its previous contract. The story did not cite specific sources and like the *Sports Business Journal* story said the NHL was also going to sign deals with Bell Media and Rogers Media, which would both take more playoff games from the CBC.

The interesting thing about that story was that it said the CBC deal "would be part of a wide-ranging agreement that ensures Saturday night and Stanley Cup finals broadcasts remain key components of CBC's programming…" This could have been a CBC person spinning the Rogers deal to sound better than it was and leaving the reporter to make his own conclusions about the rest of the story. After all, that was the part of the report that was correct.

One veteran CBC staffer, who was in contact with network management before the Rogers announcement, agreed that serious spinning was going on: "The night before, I got a text from somebody at CBC saying we kept the rights with Rogers. So I think the upper-level guys at CBC knew they were out but they kind of framed it like we kept the rights. They were trying to save face. So technically they still had the rights because the games were going to air on CBC but they didn't have the actual rights. I've always believed that's why [*The Globe and Mail*] had that story wrong, that somebody from CBC told them they kept it."

Several hours after those stories hit the street, Keith Pelley, Nadir Mohamed, Gary Bettman, Québecor president and CEO Robert Dépatie and Hubert Lacroix sat on stage in a packed theatre with the Stanley Cup perched beside them. They took turns laying out the details of the new contract. It was a 12-year deal that would see Rogers pay a total of $5.232 billion, an average of $433 million per year, to the NHL for its national Canadian broadcast rights. The revolutionary aspect of the deal was that for the first time a major professional sports league in North America sold all of its rights on all platforms to one company in a long-term deal. For its billions of dollars, Rogers won the right to show NHL games on conventional television, cable and satellite television, online via streaming and on mobile devices like iPads and smart phones. There was one exception in the first year—the national radio rights did not go to Rogers until the 2015–16 season because the existing contract with SiriusXM did not expire until then.

"It's a game-changer for sports broadcasting," said Mohamed, who moved up his departure as Rogers CEO to December in the wake of landing the contract. He added that the biggest rights contract in both Canadian and NHL history put Rogers in position to achieve its goal of beating TSN as the top sports network in Canada.

"Today's deal builds on an incredible sports legacy and solidifies our position as Canada's No. 1 sports destination," he said. "Sports content is a pillar for Rogers and NHL hockey is the holy grail. Two years ago I said I wanted Sportsnet to be the No. 1 sports brand in Canada. Today we're positioned to do just that."

Giddy is too strong a word for how Mohamed, Pelley and Bettman appeared at the press conference but they were clearly thrilled with the announcement. Bettman got off a joke about his usual reception in public from hockey fans, generally when he is presenting the Stanley Cup to the captain of the winning team. "And I didn't get booed," he said.

Both Pelley and Bettman noted the contract was a radical change from the usual rights deal because it was designed to take into account both the rapidly changing habits of young consumers, the millennials, and the equally rapid changes in the broadcasting business.

"We want a relationship where we and our partner will have the flexibility to move among platforms because people, particularly of varying ages, are consuming their entertainment differently than they ever did before and differently by age," Bettman said. "People my age [61 at the time] still rely on a big-screen TV. Our kids, my grandkids, are watching on tablets and phones. We wanted to ensure that our fans would have access to our games no matter what platform they were interested in or what platform may develop. We may be looking at things in the course of this deal that don't currently exist."

The contract gave Rogers the right to national broadcasts on Wednesdays, Saturdays and Sundays for the most part, with some games, often those between two US teams, coming on other nights. Games involving any of the seven Canadian teams could be shown across the country on those nights with no local blackouts. The big change, of course, came on Saturdays. The CBC retained its *Hockey Night in Canada* doubleheaders but it could no longer black out games by region. The other Canadian games would be shown on Rogers' networks. For example, while a Toronto Maple Leafs–Pittsburgh Penguins game was being shown on the CBC, a Montreal Canadiens–New York Rangers game would be on Sportsnet or City.

"If there are four or five games on Saturday night at the same time, no matter where you are in Canada you can flip between games," Bettman said. "You can stay on the game that you're most interested in. If one game gets out of hand and another game is going into overtime, you can watch that. That's why we're saying this is so pro-fan, because we're going to give the fan more options than they've ever had to consume NHL hockey."

Québecor bought all of the national French-language rights for its new TVA Sports network in a sub-licence deal with Rogers that would run for the entire 12 years of the NHL contract for $65 million per year.

While it was Dépatie who took the bows at the press conference, the deal was actually championed (and negotiated) by Pierre Dion, CEO of Québecor's TVA Group. Pelley and Moore probably would not have been able to sell the Rogers board on the deal without the safety net of Québecor's money, which earned Dion their eternal gratitude.

Lacroix did his best to explain the CBC's part of the deal but as the reporters in the audience read the press releases it became obvious the network was hanging on to *Hockey Night in Canada* in name only. The CBC president admitted the financial waters were simply too deep for the network. He tried to emphasize the fact that even though the CBC was handing over its prime-time airwaves for free, with Rogers taking all of the revenue from *Hockey Night*, the network was not paying a rights fee to Rogers. Thus it no longer had the risk of selling all the advertising and did not have to worry about replacing the minimum of 320 hours of programming the show represents.

"For over 60 years on Saturday night CBC has had a standing date with Canadians," Lacroix said at the press conference. "I'm comforted we will be able to see this connection live on.

"While we thought we brought something very special to broadcasting, CBC was not candidly in a position to spend taxpayers' money in this game of high stakes."

This explanation was of little comfort to many CBC employees, when it was paired with what Lacroix told them before the negotiations started. After the Harper government made the latest cuts to the CBC in 2012, Lacroix told the network's staff that renewing the agreement with the NHL was a top priority because "it's an important piece in the funding and the assumptions we have, because of what it represents in advertising revenue."

The advocacy group Friends of Canadian Broadcasting said in a report that the NHL accounted for half of the CBC's English-language advertising revenue (the network lost the French rights to RDS in 2002) and 30 per cent of its viewers. The CBC's annual ad revenue was estimated in other media reports to be around $450 million. And by 2013, despite the overall decline in television audiences, the first game of the *Hockey Night* doubleheader, usually featuring the Maple Leafs, was averaging about two million viewers. The second game drew audiences of about one million.

Neil McEneaney, the CBC's acting head of English-language services and one half of the NHL negotiating team, tried to spin the loss of the hockey revenue as no big deal, echoing one of his predecessors in his job, Richard Stursberg. "Over time, we tried to make the margins on *Hockey Night in Canada* as large as we could," he told *The Globe and Mail.* "But we had some good years and you had some years that were a function of a poor economy."

He should have added that a lot of years were a function of a poor Toronto Maple Leafs team. The Maple Leafs missed the NHL playoffs for seven consecutive seasons starting with the 2005–06 season, which followed the season lost to the lockout. That meant the CBC missed the playoff bonanza of higher ratings and higher ad revenues when the Leafs appeared in the post-season for eight years in a row.

The Leafs did give the CBC a small bonus by making the Stanley Cup tournament in the lockout-shortened 2012–13 season. The 2013 playoffs gave the CBC a tantalizing look at what was still possible when the team with the most fans was in the mix, even in the era of diminishing television audiences. Game 7 of the Leafs' first-round series against the Boston Bruins, in which they blew a 4-1 lead in the third period and lost 5-4 in overtime, drew 5.1 million viewers. This broke two CBC records—most-watched Maple Leafs playoff game and most-watched first-round game. The Toronto–Boston series was the most-watched opening-round series in CBC history with an average of 3.53 million viewers over the seven games. Alas, this was just a blip as the Leafs reverted to form in 2013–14, the final season for CBC's ownership of *Hockey Night*, and missed the playoffs again.

Shortly after the announcement, McEneaney admitted there would be layoffs in the CBC sales staff now that Rogers had control of the advertising revenue and the production staff, too, depending on how many of them would survive in the Rogers version of *Hockey Night*. But he was also doing some damage control. "But this is day one and we need to sit down and figure out exactly how Rogers wants to proceed. Outside of hockey, we're not anticipating a significant impact," McEneaney told *The Globe and Mail.*

Considering the CBC had just lost half of its advertising revenue, that last sentence raised more than a few eyebrows.

Lacroix, who looked uncomfortable in the extreme during his time on the Rogers stage, tried to play up the idea the CBC would not pay Rogers any rights fees for *Hockey Night* and would not be taking the risk of selling enough advertising to turn a profit. But this overlooked the fact the CBC would actually be paying Rogers a good portion of the production costs through cash payments, assigning its own technical staff to the show and providing studio and office space rent-free. And, of course, the surrender of CBC's prime-time schedule on Saturdays and almost every night during the playoffs for free.

In a memo to CBC employees that went out at the same time as the Rogers press conference, Lacroix said much the same but also was honest when it came to the possibility of lost jobs. He admitted, "this isn't the outcome we hoped for," and went on to say, "While this deal will result in job losses, the staffing impact would have been much greater had we lost hockey entirely, as CBC is still producing hockey."

The memo went out in advance of a town-hall meeting at the CBC's Front Street headquarters. Lacroix, Orridge and McEneaney appeared in front of the CBC's head-office staff and it was not a happy event. Some of those in attendance said there was open grumbling that Lacroix should resign and in the months to come at other CBC town halls, Lacroix would hear that sentiment openly directed at him.

Meanwhile, at the Rogers headquarters a few dozen blocks uptown, Pelley was in a swirl of mixed emotions. Although he was overjoyed at engineering such a coup, he was also as nervous as he was in the moments leading up to Bettman's decision to go with Rogers. All he had on paper for the contract was the brief memorandum of understanding that was signed by all parties a couple of days previously.

"We announced on that Tuesday and although we had that binding MOU [memorandum of understanding], [the contract] was subject to the NHL board of governors' approval," Pelley said. "The NHL governors could have voted against it."

Technically, that is true. Every major decision Gary Bettman makes is subject to approval by the NHL's team owners. But Bettman is brilliant when it comes to handling his bosses. He does all the necessary lobbying and convincing behind closed doors in advance of any vote. No vote is called until Bettman decides he has his ducks properly lined up, which is why almost all the votes are announced as unanimous. It was and still is unheard of for the governors to reject anything put in front of them by Bettman. Pelley was well aware of this, but given the size of the stakes he could not help but be nervous until the contract received the official stamp of approval on December 9, 2013, at the governors' annual winter meetings in Pebble Beach, California.

As he discovered later, Pelley had good reason to be concerned. George Cope, the CEO of Bell Canada, as noted previously, plays hard. And he had a change of heart. Cope, who sources said did not act a few days earlier when he was tipped off about the Rogers play for the NHL contract, decided to use the 13 days until the governors' meeting to try and get Bell back in the game.

The first thing Cope did, according to multiple sources, was fly down to New York a few days after the Rogers press conference for a meeting with Bettman. Apparently he was told Bell's bid did not measure up to Rogers' because there were too many demands like a priority on scheduling. Bettman, sources said, elected not to tell him his absence from the talks did not help matters. Cope also put more money on the table, although sources said he did not merely raise the $5.2-billion bid Bell put in earlier. This time he suggested to Bettman that the commissioner should create some room for Bell to get a set of games in addition to Rogers. The combined money from both companies would then top the billions the NHL was going to get from Rogers starting in 2014.

Bettman declined the offer but Cope wasn't finished. He decided to lobby at least a few NHL governors to intercede for him with Bettman with an eye to postponing the vote. Apparently, the idea was to get enough time to talk Bettman into giving Bell a piece of the action. A couple of sources said Cope actually showed up in Pebble Beach to lobby some governors in person.

Cope's lobbying raises an interesting question about MLSE chairman and Leafs governor Larry Tanenbaum. His role in this is not known and no one was interested in talking about it, including Tanenbaum. He declined a request for comment placed through an MLSE executive. But it must have been an uncomfortable time for Tanenbaum given the hard feelings about the broadcast deal between his two partners in MLSE.

The agenda for the governors' meeting called for Pelley to address the board and explain the deal. Then the governors would discuss the contract among themselves and cast their votes. Given Pelley's admitted nervousness going into the meeting, the butterflies must have really started churning in his stomach when Bettman called him at 7:00 a.m. on the morning of December 9 at the governors' hotel. He told Pelley he needed to speak to him and told him to come down for breakfast.

Bettman said there was something Pelley needed to know: George Cope was in town and was lobbying governors in an attempt to postpone or even change the vote. However, Bettman added, there was nothing for Pelley to worry about. All he had to do was make his presentation to the governors, leave the room and then there would be a discussion followed by a vote.

Back in Toronto, Sportsnet president Scott Moore was monitoring the situation from home. This is where all the relationships he built with the Canadian NHL governors going back to his days with the CBC came into play. Pelley spent about 45 minutes talking to the governors and then left the room and sat outside. The discussion among the governors started and some of them began texting Moore about what was being said.

"Having those relationships with the Canadian governors really helped," Moore said. "Because Keith went down [to Pebble Beach] and he's sitting outside the room. I'm back in my condo and I'm getting texts from the meeting saying Bell's put more money on the table. But Gary said, 'This is my deal, I stand behind my deal. Bell had their chance and Rogers are going to be better partners.' "

When the vote was called, it went the way all votes go in the Bettman regime, 29-0 in favour. The contract was approved, technically by a unanimous vote. "I knew the vote before Gary came out and told Keith," Moore said, referring to the governors who were texting him. "But we were both sweating. You don't know if Gary's going to live up to the deal because in the deal it says subject to the board of governors' approval.

"It goes back to speaking to Gary's credibility and his ethics. You can talk about being a tough guy to negotiate with and I've negotiated several things with him on different things. The reality is he negotiates hard and once you're his partner, you're his partner."

There were only 29 votes cast because Larry Tanenbaum, representing the Maple Leafs, abstained. There were a couple of stories put forward on that. One came from a column by Damien Cox in the *Toronto Star*. He wrote that Bettman persuaded Tanenbaum to abstain because he planned to vote against the deal in the wake of an acrimonious MLSE board meeting where the Bell and Rogers representatives were said to have clashed over the new rights contract. Rather than spoil a unanimous vote with a ballot that would not make any difference, Bettman was supposed to have talked Tanenbaum out of voting.

If indeed Tanenbaum planned to vote against the deal this would have raised many questions about where he stood with Cope's lobbying efforts.

However, after Cox's column appeared, I wrote a follow-up story about the vote for *The Globe and Mail*. In talking to several NHL and MLSE sources, I was told that Tanenbaum himself decided to abstain from the vote. His decision came after a consultation with Dale Lastman, who does double duty as Tanenbaum's lawyer and a member of MLSE's board of directors. The issue was the Leafs had a conflict of interest in the matter because the vote concerned a contract that involved the NHL conferring a benefit to one of their owners.

A great postscript on the governors' vote came from Richard Peddie, the former president and CEO of MLSE who retired in December 2011. In an interview with the *National Post*, he laughed at the idea there was any chance the governors would take the time out from their annual sojourn to the sunny climes of either California or Florida (the meetings alternated between the two states), to examine the broadcast contract thoroughly and perhaps vote against it.

"Oh, that is the meeting where less work gets done," Peddie said. "You go down there, and you have some little light meeting on the Monday afternoon, and something in the [Tuesday] morning. All the rich owners are flying out in their private jets, and they don't want to hang around. So little work gets done."

But what about the big vote on the contract? "The horse is already out of the barn. And there's a big number called five billion on the table. So it's a little tough to vote against."

7

QUÉBECOR GETS IN THE GAME

If there is one detail those involved in the great rights negotiations of 2013 agree on, it is that Rogers never could have snatched the NHL broadcast rights out from under Bell if Québecor Inc. had not signed on to sub-license the French-language rights. At first glance, this looks almost like a minor deal given the overall $5.2-billion price tag on the Rogers-NHL contract but there are several strands to this important story, each one of them compelling in its own right.

When Pierre Dion agreed to a sub-licence for all 12 years of the Rogers deal that started at $125 million per year, it gave Keith Pelley enough of a financial cushion to persuade his bosses to commit $5.2 billion. Dion, who by all accounts is a self-effacing businessman, was said to have championed the deal within Québecor as enthusiastically as Pelley did with Edward Rogers and Nadir Mohamed and the Rogers board of directors.

"He may be very modest about his impact but from my point of view, Rogers never gets there without Pierre," John Collins said. "His willingness to spend on the French national rights and the gap between what he was willing to spend and what Bell and RDS was willing to spend, is what really made the deal for Rogers. It gave them the ability, because they didn't have the infrastructure to generate as much revenue as Bell was going to do, that gave them the ability to do it."

The first strand in the French rights story is Québecor's financial commitment on behalf of its new and aggressive TVA Sports network. By subtracting the company's payment from what Rogers agreed to pay the NHL, Pelley could say—and often did if any of his rivals from Bell were around—that Rogers was actually paying less than what Bell offered the NHL. A lot less, in fact, which is something few people outside the broadcasting business realize. Once you do the math, it turned a $5.2-billion commitment to the NHL into one closer to $3.7 billion, which explains why Edward Rogers and the board bought in. If Bell had won the rights deal, it would not have been able to find the same cushion because the French rights would have gone to RDS, its own network.

"I would not have been able to get my own board's approval if we had not had [TVA Sports]," Pelley said.

When Pelley told Gary Bettman in September 2013 he was interested in bidding on the gatekeeper model of the rights, he knew one of the most important things he had to do was find someone to sub-license the French rights. RDS, which held the French national and Montreal Canadiens' regional rights ever since there were such things, was obviously out of the question. Pelley and Moore briefly toyed with the idea of starting their own French sports network but that was put aside after the first conversation with Dion.

TVA Sports was launched in September 2011 by Québecor. It started out with a deal with Rogers for production help and to sub-license some of Rogers' content, which made it a natural partner for the French-language NHL rights. Since TVA was doing what Rogers Media itself was doing, aggressively pursuing content in order to challenge its more established rival in the ratings and subscription war, Pelley found a receptive listener in TVA CEO Pierre Dion.

Dion and Pelley agreed to a deal that saw TVA commit $125 million per year for the first half of the Rogers deal, rising to $130 million for the final six years. But it was actually two deals in one. The French-language national rights would cost $65 million per year. For that, TVA Sports got 22 Montreal Canadiens regular-season games plus their playoff games, other NHL playoff games, the all-star game, Winter Classic and the Stanley Cup final. TVA also obtained the same digital rights as Rogers did. The other $60 million was for the Canadiens' regional package, which was their other 60 regular-season games. That deal expired at the same time as the CBC's national NHL contract at the end of the 2013–14 season, which meant they came up for auction at the same time as the national deal. Dion guaranteed TVA Sports would bid $60 million per year for 12 years for the Habs' regional games.

The Canadiens' French regional rights actually went into negotiations earlier in 2013 with Bell Media. However, Bell was not offering the kind of money Canadiens owner Geoff Molson and Bettman wanted. The stalemate led to the meeting where George Cope had a confrontation with Bettman, further damaging an already tense relationship. After that contentious meeting, both Bell and the NHL agreed to postpone the French-language negotiations until the Canadian national package was settled.

If TVA failed to land the Canadiens' regional rights, Rogers agreed to reduce its annual payment for the sub-licence to $65 million. This clause was necessary because RDS had the right, under its contract with the Canadiens, to match any new offer for the regional French-language rights and hold on to them. Going into the negotiations, Bell Media had the same attitude it had toward the national English package, that there was little chance of any competition.

At that point, according to one broadcasting source, RDS was in the same position as its sister network TSN was in the years leading up to the founding of Sportsnet in 1998. "It had a nice, comfortable monopoly," the source said. Until TVA Sports came on the scene in late 2011, RDS was the only player when it came to French-language rights. Thus it could practically dictate the prices, which certainly helped RDS's bottom line. By the time TVA Sports arrived, RDS was good for a steady pre-tax profit of between $20 million and more than $40 million per year, according to Canadian Radio-television and Telecommunications Commission (CRTC) figures.

The reason Bell Media did not consider TVA Sports serious competition is that in its first two years of operation, 2012 and 2013, it lost a total of $40 million according to the CRTC. Also, TVA had a mere 1.6 million subscribers in 2012, compared to RDS's 3.5 million. And the CRTC listed RDS as turning a profit of $25.7 million in 2012.

One thing should be noted about the CRTC's financial numbers on Canada's television networks—they are based on numbers submitted by the network owners in certain categories requested by the CRTC. However, the owners use some of the numbers differently in their own annual financial statements so the CRTC figures should be considered more of an indication of financial health rather than an accurate calculation.

"Gary Bettman loved the fact, as did Geoff Molson, of bringing another player into the marketplace," a broadcast source said of TVA Sports' emergence on the scene in 2011. As they did with the Canadian national English rights, Bettman and John Collins set about researching what the French-language regional and national rights would be worth with a second network in the bidding. They also had help from Molson and Kevin Gilmore, the team's chief operating officer.

"There was a lot of work done with Geoff Molson and Kevin Gilmore to really flush out the value," Collins said. "Talk about the most important content anywhere—the Montreal Canadiens in Québec. We valued the regional rights of the Canadiens at a certain level based on a lot of the work we had seen with other regional deals in other markets, not just Canadian markets but in the US, iconic clubs' rights-holders."

Collins said there was some consideration given to the Canadiens launching their own regional network but that, like Rogers' flirtation with the idea, did not last long.

Once talks began with Bell Media there were problems. Aside from the company's reluctance to pay what the NHL was looking for, George Cope told Collins and Bettman since BCE was an 18-per-cent owner of the Canadiens, its RDS subsidiary should get greater consideration as the regional rights-holder. He was not happy about Québecor getting in on the action.

Cope, CTV president Phil King and RDS president Gerry Frappier made it clear there was a ceiling on the rights fees for them. "I don't want to say there was a real disconnect," Collins said. "It was another instance where we just couldn't agree on value. While there was no disagreement about the power of Canadian rights in those markets or French rights to the NHL, there was another situation where we can only pay you what we can pay you.

"It was nowhere near what we wanted individually for each one of the packages or collectively. So we didn't get to an agreement. And it had been a year where we were discussing this. There was an agreement to table it until we had the national rights discussions because that's probably where it would be best discussed."

This left the rights still open for bids, and Pelley and Dion stepped up in the fall of 2013. By guaranteeing he would bid on the Habs' regional rights for $60 million per year plus pay $65 million per year for the national French-language rights, Dion made a commitment of $125 million to $130 million a year for 12 years that came off what Rogers would have to pay. TVA's total obligation over 12 years works out to $1.53 billion. Subtract that from the $5.232 billion Rogers was going to pay and it is $3.702 billion. That number was a much easier sell to Edward Rogers and his fellow Rogers directors.

Once TVA Sports' commitment was known, in November 2013, Bell had to decide if it wanted to match its bid on the Canadiens' regional rights. In the previous contract, with no competing bidders, RDS paid $20 million per year for both the national French rights and the Canadiens' regional French rights. This represented a three-fold jump in price for fewer games, which set off a fierce internal debate at Bell Canada. Some executives argued it made no sense to triple what they paid because it would wipe out RDS's profit. In the end, the decision was to match TVA's bid so that RDS could keep the regional French rights.

"It was a significant profit reset," Frappier admitted to *The Globe and Mail*, although he insisted the network remains profitable. The CRTC showed RDS going from a pre-tax profit of $45.4 million in 2014, the final year of the previous contract, to $19.9 million in 2015.

The interesting part of the TVA–RDS battle is the NHL is still giving Rogers credit for a full $1.53 billion off the contract price of $5.2 billion even though $720 million is being paid by Bell for the Habs' regional rights. That is essentially a payoff due to the NHL's gratitude to Pierre Dion and Québecor forcing a 300-per-cent increase in the price of the Canadiens' regional French rights and getting it $125 million per year out of the Québec market. In essence, Rogers and TVA Sports produced an increase of more than

$100 million per year in revenue for the NHL because previously RDS paid just $20 million for both the Canadiens' regional French rights and the national French rights.

Part of the regional rights money goes to the team and part goes to the league (the exact split is not known). However, all of the regional money is counted in the NHL's annual hockey-related revenue (HRR). HRR is the total revenues of the league and its 31 teams. That is split 50-50 with the players according to the collective agreement. Hence as far as the league is concerned, once Pelley got Québecor to commit, it was getting a total of $5.2 billion for the national and Habs' French rights (which were always sold as one in previous years) so it didn't matter where the actual cash came from, the party that created the increase was rewarded. So in a sense, Bell Media is paying part of the freight of Rogers' NHL deal through its RDS subsidiary.

Collins felt postponing the Canadiens' French rights discussions earlier in 2013 was a key move because when they resumed, the English and French national rights were also up for bids, which raised prices all around.

"Having gone through the French-Canadian rights negotiations prior to that we knew what the market would bear," Collins said. "So the ability to put English and French together really benefited the regional package for the Canadiens, because at that point RDS was going to pay whatever they had to pay to make sure they kept the Canadiens, but it also drove the value of the bigger English deal.

"That was the thing I don't think Bell saw coming. I think everybody underestimated TVA's contribution to the deal. That gave Rogers equal footing with Bell from a financial standpoint. That's the kind of guy Pierre [Dion] is. He basically let Rogers and Keith [Pelley] make the deal."

Even though TVA Sports did not manage to snatch the Habs' French rights away from RDS, it did land some serious punches on its rival. By grabbing the French-language national rights, which included the Canadiens' playoff games, TVA gained a foothold in the Québec market for the first time. And by forcing RDS to triple what it paid for the Canadiens' rights, TVA put a serious dent in its rival's ability to pay for other programming, just as it arrived to drive up the prices for said programming. Holding the French rights also gave TVA the power to tell advertisers they needed to buy time on less popular networks owned by Québecor if they wanted to advertise on Canadiens' games, a strategy long employed by the CBC when it had *Hockey Night in Canada*.

"It will increase our number of subscribers to TVA Sports," Dion told *The Globe and Mail*. "And it will allow us to market a unique advertising offer through our [all-news] TVA network LCN and other chains. This is all part of our bigger business plan."

Bettman was no stranger to this kind of manoeuvring. The dance with Pelley, TVA and RDS was much the same as the one the NHL commissioner did about 15 years earlier when he used the arrival of Sportsnet to create more revenue for his league. And just like TVA Sports, Sportsnet owes its place on the Canadian broadcasting landscape to Bettman's willingness to take its money.

TSN's share of the Canadian national English NHL rights expired after the 1997–98 season. Sportsnet was then known as CTV Sportsnet and launched in 1998 as a joint venture between CTV, Liberty Media and Rogers. This was before Bell Canada Enterprises bought, sold and then reacquired CTV (selling Sportsnet was ordered by the CRTC as a condition of the purchase). In order to establish itself with Canadian viewers, Sportsnet needed properties they would watch, so when TSN's share of the NHL rights came up for bids the new network was ready for action.

A familiar scenario came into play when Gary Bettman told TSN it had competition for the first time with the NHL package. Broadcasting legend Gordon Craig, the founding president of

TSN, refused to take the newcomer seriously. Craig, according to a source with knowledge of the negotiations, dug in when Bettman asked for more than the $10 million TSN annually paid in the previous contract. The TSN boss did not think Sportsnet posed a serious threat. But the new network offered $15 million (yes, rights fees have certainly taken off in the last 20 years) and was off to the races with its first major programming coup while TSN had to do without a national NHL package for the next four seasons.

"In hindsight that was one of the smartest moves Gary Bettman ever did. They launched Sportsnet on the back of the NHL," said someone who was involved in the change from TSN to Sportsnet. "So he's already been through this story before. Now he brought this history through [TVA Sports]. What he did was create another player in the marketplace. That's what he did with this again. He upped the regional rights, upped the national rights and put another player in the market."

Bettman's coup did come at a cost for some viewers across Canada. With a second French-language sports network on the scene, the NHL suddenly enforced a blackout rule concerning the Canadiens' games that it never had in the previous 25 years. Up until the 2014–15 season, RDS was the only carrier of French-language Canadiens broadcasts. So the national French rights were always part of the regional package and since there were relatively few francophone viewers west of Eastern Ontario, the NHL considered the value of the contract to be on the regional side. The league did not mind if RDS carried all of the Canadiens' games on its national feed, which meant thousands of fans in Canada, west of the Habs' broadcast region of a small slice of Eastern Ontario, Québec and Atlantic Canada, were able to watch the Canadiens in French. Each team's region is elastic when two or more teams are close together. Each team has an 80-kilometre radius around its city to itself but can share a region with another team outside of that. This mainly concerns the Canadiens and the Ottawa

Senators, who share their broadcast region, which means both their games can be seen.

However, once TVA Sports came on the scene and established a real value for the French-language national NHL rights, Bettman ruled it was time to enforce the regional blackouts. Those black-outs exist to protect the value of each team's regional broadcast rights. The NHL believes, for example, if it allowed too many Maple Leafs games to be broadcast in the Winnipeg Jets' region that would hurt the value of the Jets' regional rights.

Between 38 and 60 games of each of the seven Canadian NHL teams are designated as regional games for both English and French broadcasts. If one carrier is both the national and regional rights-holder for a team, which would be Rogers under the current NHL deal, it can designate more games as national games. For example, Rogers does this in the case of the Edmonton Oilers, since their superstar Connor McDavid is a big ratings attraction across the country. But if, in the example of the Winnipeg Jets and Ottawa Senators, the team's regional rights are held by TSN, then fewer games are designated as national games.

With the French national and regional rights now held by two different broadcasters, the affected francophone viewers and anglophone Canadiens fans had to reach into their wallets. They could buy a cable or satellite package that carried both RDS and TVA Sports and thus see all 82 Habs games plus the playoffs in French or they could buy a specialty package like NHL Centre Ice French, which was Rogers' response to viewers who lost the RDS national games. That costs about $60 per season but it's only available if the local cable company offers it. Another choice is a streaming service like Rogers' GameCentre Live, which also has a French version for $60 and a TV provider is not needed to get it. Or the more expensive ($200 per season) NHL Centre Ice cable or satellite package is also a solution.

"It's a unique situation," Frappier told *The Globe and Mail*. "A French broadcast going into Alberta wasn't bothering anybody. Given there weren't two competing players sharing rights, there was no reason for anyone to enforce the rights. So [the NHL] gave us a free ride. All they're doing [now] is enforcing the rules."

TVA Sports saw an immediate result from landing the national French rights. There was a 20-per-cent jump in the network's subscribers in one year, climbing to two million in 2015. But TVA was still plagued by cord-cutters like every other broadcaster. According to the most recent CRTC numbers, TVA's subscribers dropped by 6.2 per cent in 2016 to 1.9 million.

Profits remained elusive for Québecor and TVA Sports until the 2017 NHL playoffs when the Canadian teams finally made a good showing. Dion predicted it would take at least five years for the NHL deal to become profitable and he was proved right thanks to the Canadian teams. In its 2017 second-quarter results, Québecor said TVA Sports drove an improvement in the media division's profit. Québecor Media's operating income went up 121.7 per cent in 2017 over the same period in 2016, climbing to $15.3 million. The company said this was due to greater subscription and advertising revenues at both TVA Sports and the TVA network. The 2017 Stanley Cup final between the Pittsburgh Penguins and the Nashville Predators drew an average audience of 962,000, which was the best in Québec since 2008.

On the programming front, TVA Sports did make gains on RDS in the years after getting the national French NHL rights. It managed to steal the NFL, some Major League Baseball and tennis away from RDS, along with the Major League Soccer and Montreal Impact French-language rights in 2017. But the increased expenses meant the network itself was still not profitable. In 2016, according to the CRTC's numbers, TVA Sports lost $33.1 million, probably because the cost of rights fees alone had jumped to $73.4 million from $5.7 million in 2013, just before the NHL deal kicked in.

In the meantime, RDS may have taken a kick in the slats when its profit dipped by more than 50 per cent in 2015 to $19.9 million but it remained in the black since then. According to the CRTC, RDS's profit rose 38.2 per cent in 2016 to $27.5 million.

While the losses at TVA Sports may seem daunting, another strand in this story is that there is a reason Québecor is quite willing to keep pumping money into the network. Aside from challenging RDS for the top spot among Québec sports viewers, an equal or even greater motivation for Québecor's executives was their desire to land an NHL team for Québec City, which has been without one since the Nordiques left in 1995 to become the Colorado Avalanche.

Pierre Karl Péladeau, the controlling shareholder of Québecor who stepped down as CEO for four years from 2013 to early 2017 for an ill-fated try at politics, has been pursuing an NHL team for years. He threw the resources of Québecor behind the bid. The company was the driving force behind the building of the state-of-the-art arena in Québec City, which seats 18,259 and cost $370 million to build. It opened on September 8, 2015, in the hope an NHL team will come along in a few years. Québecor bought the management rights and the naming rights—it's called the Videotron Centre after the company's telecommunications wing, which offers cable, wireless and Internet services. In exchange for those rights, Québecor is paying $33 million per year in rent. If an NHL team comes along, the rent rises to $63.5 million.

Péladeau's strategy in pursuing a team is not new to the NHL. Indeed, it is a time-honoured way to gain entrance, going back more than 50 years to the days of the six-team league, for the NHL is in fact more of a private club than a traditional business. Entry is strictly controlled by the existing owners and only those who are willing to dance to their tune—which generally means handing over large amounts of cash to the league—are admitted. This was something BlackBerry billionaire Jim Balsillie refused to acknowledge. It cost him millions of dollars in three attempts to force the NHL to allow him to buy a team and move it to Hamilton before he finally admitted defeat in the wake of the Phoenix Coyotes bankruptcy saga.

By shipping hundreds of millions of dollars the NHL's way through his television network, Péladeau is proving to the NHL he will be a good partner. Prospective owners who drag the league through the courts, airing dirty laundry and costing it millions in legal and other costs, have the door slammed in their faces.

Some years ago, an NHL governor explained what Péladeau was doing and drew a line from him back to Seymour and Northrup Knox, the original owners of the Buffalo Sabres. It was a fascinating tale about how this system works—the usual quid pro quo method used in any business but with lots of twists and turns.

In 1965, with the NHL planning to double in size by adding six expansion teams, the Knox brothers wanted to get one of the teams for Buffalo. The city already had a long-standing and successful American Hockey League team in the Buffalo Bisons with a large fan base. With the well-heeled Knox brothers as prospective owners, making Buffalo one of the new teams seemed almost automatic.

However, in the 1960s the NHL was still a bush-league, incestuous operation that saw the Norris family control as many as three of the six franchises. A contemptuous nickname for the league used to be the "Norris House League." For a long time, the family name adorned the Norris Division when divisions were named for prominent NHL owners and executives. But those wanting to buy into the NHL had to win over the Norris brothers—Bruce, who inherited the Detroit Red Wings, and the notorious Jim, who was part-owner of the Chicago Blackhawks and controlled the New York Rangers through his ownership of Madison Square Garden. Jim Norris was infamous thanks to his ownership of the International Boxing Club, which controlled professional boxing in the 1950s and was linked to organized crime. But the league still presents the James Norris Trophy to its best defenceman every year.

According to various media reports, Seymour and Northrup Knox made an excellent presentation to the NHL owners in their pursuit of a team. But Jim Norris was said to have told them Buffalo would never get a team because it wasn't a major-league city. He supposedly lost $2 million some years earlier in a grain venture in Buffalo and remained angry about it.

When the new teams were announced in February 1966, Buffalo was not among them. But St. Louis was, even though there was no owner for the team. Funny thing, though—Jim Norris just happened to own the St. Louis Arena. The Knox brothers were stunned, not to mention angry. Also making the cut were the Oakland Seals, who had 52 owners with Barry van Gerbig as the front man. Van Gerbig, who once played goal for Princeton University, did not have a lot of money but he was pals with a few NHL owners. That made him more qualified to own an NHL team than the Knox brothers, but he did pave their way into the NHL.

The Seals were a disaster from the start. Few people in the Bay Area watched their games. Even though some of the 52 owners, like Bing Crosby, had money, none of them were willing to spend it on the team. By March 1968, the Seals accepted a $680,000 loan from Labatt Brewing Company. The brewery wanted to move the Seals to Vancouver and the team had to pay off the loan in less than one year if it were to stay in Oakland. However, the NHL had a television deal with CBS at the time and the network did not want to lose the large Oakland–San Francisco TV market even if nobody was watching.

Bill Jennings, the president of the New York Rangers, called Seymour Knox and asked him to put money into the Seals to keep them alive for the 1968–69 season. The payoff might be to move the team to Buffalo the following season. Eventually, a deal was struck that would see the Knox brothers finance the Seals and then apply to buy and move them to Buffalo for the 1969–70 season.

The problem was, Labatt screamed bloody murder once the deal became known. It appears NHL president Clarence Campbell did not make sure things were worked out with Labatt once the league owners decided to take the Knox money. After a long period of discussions, during which it became clear moving the Seals out of Oakland was still not an option to CBS, it was agreed Seymour and Northrup Knox would buy the Seals but without a promise of getting a team for Buffalo. But they would now be in the NHL owners' club and free to persuade their new peers to see things their way.

By December 1969, the Knox brothers not only found a buyer for most of their interest in the Seals but they were awarded one of two expansion teams and the Buffalo Sabres were born. The other expansion team was the Vancouver Canucks. The Seals would undergo name changes, many ownership adventures and a move before they folded in 1978 as the Cleveland Barons and were merged with the Minnesota North Stars. It isn't known what the Knox brothers' net investment in the Seals was—it was at least $1 million and probably a lot more—but keeping them alive gave them the chance to spend the then astronomical price of $6 million on an expansion team for their hometown.

"Seymour and Norty put money into Oakland to keep that team alive," the NHL governor said. "Then they got their reward with the team in Buffalo."

There were other examples over the years of owners helping themselves after good service to the league—Craig Leipold managed to sell the money-losing Nashville Predators (at the time) in 2008 and upgrade to the Minnesota Wild, which played to full houses—but none will have spent as much as Péladeau if he ever manages to get a team for Québec City. John Collins, the now-former NHL chief operating officer, says Péladeau can thank

Pierre Dion, who was eventually promoted to president and CEO of Québecor, for that plus clearing the way for Rogers to get the NHL broadcasting rights.

"He's a class guy who obviously wants a team to Québec City," Collins said of Dion. "So he's playing by the rules and doing everything he can to be a good partner with the league." That did not prevent Dion from losing his post as Québecor CEO when Péladeau returned to the company in February 2017. He was bumped to chairman of Québecor Media but also given $7.2 million in severance pay.

The problem is, being a good partner with the league does not guarantee a team is going to be delivered to you. Gary Bettman made that clear when the Rogers deal was announced and several reporters tried to connect the dots between Péladeau's company spending hundreds of millions of dollars on the French rights, his deals with the arena in Québec City and an NHL team.

"The dots are not connectable," Bettman said. "One has nothing to do with the other right now."

Then the commissioner issued his boilerplate response that comes whenever someone asks if the league will be adding any teams in Canada: "It's not something we're embarking on in a formal process. We've had expressions of interest from a number of places but it's not something we have any intention of addressing in the short-term."

When the league did embark on a formal expansion process, in 2016, Québecor gave it a good try but remained a bridesmaid. The company drew on former Canadian prime minister Brian Mulroney, Québecor's chairman, to woo the NHL's owners. Mulroney told them Québec City may be the smallest urban centre by population (500,000) if it is admitted to the league but its local economy and corporate community are much stronger than they were in 1995 when former owner Marcel Aubut sold the Nordiques to Stan Kroenke, who moved them to Denver.

Alas, the NHL decided in June 2016 to award just one expansion franchise, to Las Vegas for a mere $500 million (US). The Québec hopefuls were undone by two things: the unwillingness of Bettman and the owners to add a 17th team to the Eastern Conference and by a weak Canadian dollar. The latter reason was bitterly ironic, as it was the wobbly loonie in the mid-1990s, dipping into the 70-cent US range, that resulted in the Winnipeg Jets and the Nordiques heading south.

When the Rogers-NHL deal was announced on November 26, 2013, the Canadian dollar was worth 95 cents US. At the time, it was in a long, healthy run that saw it even rise above the US dollar for a while before weakening commodity and energy prices drove it down to the 80-cent range by the time of the expansion decision.

The NHL was also grappling with the geographical balance between conferences. Before Las Vegas joined the party there were 16 teams in the Eastern Conference and 14 in the Western Conference. Bettman and the owners preferred to go to 15 in the west and leave the east at 16 for fewer scheduling headaches. Their long-term goal, something no governor wants to talk about on the record, is a 32-team league with 16 teams in each conference.

However, Péladeau and Québecor did not have the door slammed in their faces. The governors said their expansion bid was not rejected, just "deferred."

"Québec's on our radar screen," Bettman said following the decision. "We know there's potential ownership, we know there's an arena and we know that there's a lot of passionate fans in the market. But the circumstances at this point in time for the reasons we articulated, it didn't make it a possible reality.

"Having said that, that's why the recommendation was not to say no, but to say in effect not right now."

Pierre Dion noted the fans had been waiting 21 years for a team to replace the Nordiques and they were all prepared to wait a bit longer. That isn't to say Dion and his fellow executives weren't disappointed.

"Of course we are, just like the fans in Québec and Québec City," Dion said. "But at the same time we understand the process. All the conditions have to be there if you want to make it a success. That's why we need to be patient and timing has to be right. We lost the Nordiques once, we don't want to lose them twice. What I can tell you is I'm confident the Nordiques will be back eventually."

A lot of NHL insiders think Québec City's best chance is to get a relocated NHL team. Relocation is always a reluctant choice by the NHL, mainly because expansion fees are much, much higher than relocation fees. The Vegas Golden Knights paid $500 million (US) to join the league for the 2017–18 season. When David Thomson and Mark Chipman bought the Atlanta Thrashers in 2011 and moved them to Winnipeg, the relocation fee was $60 million (US).

Seattle is the preferred expansion target of the mostly American NHL owners now and it took the lead in the hunt in December 2017. First, former MLSE CEO Tim Leiweke's Los Angeles-based Oak View Group had its $660-million (US) plan to renovate the existing KeyArena with private funding approved by Seattle city council. Then Gary Bettman announced the NHL gave the Seattle group permission to file an expansion application for the 2020–21 season. The new price for an expansion team was set at a cool $650 million (US). Leiweke has a deal with private-equity billionaire David Bonderman and Hollywood producer Jerry Bruckheimer to own the team.

"That doesn't mean we have granted an expansion team," Bettman told reporters. "We have agreed as a league to take and consider an expansion application and to let them run in the next few months a season-ticket drive."

Québec City now finds itself in the same position Winnipeg was for a number of years until the Thrashers were moved north in

2011. With eager, wealthy owners and an NHL-ready arena in place, Winnipeg was used by Bettman to threaten reluctant cities into granting owner-friendly arena leases to their teams or simply to cough up money to keep money-losing franchises like the Coyotes from moving. Québec must now endure the same tantalizing fate until a team, probably an Eastern Conference team, runs out of money and prospective owners and has to move. However, Bettman has shown over the years he will fight fiercely to prevent a team from moving, with the Coyotes as the prime example.

Also, as long as Québec City remains open, Bettman can put off those pushing for a second team in the Greater Toronto Area, an issue that surfaces regularly. He can always say a second team for Southern Ontario has to take a back seat to giving Québec another shot at the NHL. There is a belief the Maple Leafs might have a veto on a second team under the NHL's constitution but this has long been denied by the commissioner. All it takes is a two-thirds majority vote by the governors. The Maple Leafs' public position is that if the governors propose a second team in their region they will study the proposal and then decide where they stand. However, few believe the Leafs would willingly surrender their grip on the largest, richest hockey market in the league without a long, expensive legal war, one that would give even Bettman pause.

By late 2017, the best candidates for relocation were the usual suspects. The Coyotes were drowning in debt as always with an under-financed owner, although their presence in the Western Conference as well as Bettman's antipathy to moving them work against Péladeau. And if they do have to move, Houston emerged as a potential western destination when Tilman Fertitta, the owner of the NBA's Houston Rockets, announced his interest in a team in November 2017 and met with Bettman. In the Eastern Conference, the Florida Panthers remain a money pit, with a series of owners eventually tiring of writing cheques as large as $20 million (US) to cover annual losses. However, their current owner, billionaire Vincent Viola, who made his considerable fortune in electronic stock trading, is a hockey fan who has yet to show any fatigue over the losses.

The New York Islanders and Carolina Hurricanes, two other long-time financial basket cases, were taken out of the running, at least for now. Islander owners Jon Ledecky and Scott Malkin won approval for their $1-billion bid to build an 18,000-seat arena and a hotel among other things on the grounds of Belmont Park, the famous horse-racing track east of Manhattan. That will bring them a lot closer to their long-time fan base on Long Island after the team moved from their arena in Nassau County to Brooklyn in 2015. But it was an unhappy marriage, as Brooklyn's Barclays Center is unsuitable for hockey, with its sightlines reducing capacity to less than 15,000. The company that owns the arena is losing money as the team's landlord because it agreed to pay the Islanders $53.5 million per year in exchange for the revenue from their business operations. The Hurricanes ceased to be a possibility when Dallas billionaire Tom Dundon bought a majority share of the team from Pete Karmanos and said the team will stay in Raleigh.

One last obstacle some NHL observers see as blocking Québecor's path to a team is Péladeau's political leaning. He is a Québec separatist and took a four-year timeout from Québecor to serve as a Parti Québécois member in the National Assembly of Québec. Péladeau became party leader in May 2015 in the wake of a resounding defeat in the provincial election but resigned a year later. Péladeau returned in February 2017 as the CEO of Québecor.

Some think Péladeau would not be welcomed as an NHL owner because of his separatist views, especially since Montreal Canadiens owner Geoff Molson belongs to one of the oldest and most powerful anglo and federalist families in the province. However, money is the language of the NHL and Péladeau is circulating enough of it around the league, not to mention with the Canadiens, for his political views to be no problem at all.

8

STORMING THE CBC'S GATES

Broadcast-rights deals are won and lost all the time, with the shows in question simply shifting to the winning network. But it was unprecedented for the victors to literally storm the losers' headquarters and take over their offices.

So it went on June 1, 2014, when the forces from Rogers moved into the eighth floor of the CBC's headquarters on Front Street in downtown Toronto. In the eyes of the demoralized CBC Sports staff, already hard hit by layoffs due to funding cuts by the federal government, the barbarians were actually at the gate. It was all part of the deal between Rogers, the new owner of *Hockey Night in Canada*, and the CBC, which lost the rights to the Canadian institution after 62 years.

In exchange for continuing to air the show on Saturday nights, the CBC agreed to let Rogers sell all of the advertising time and keep the revenue plus give them office and studio space in their own building rent-free and provide the technical staff for the show plus pay their salaries. In addition to the technical staff, the on-air crews—familiar faces like Ron MacLean, play-by-play man Jim Hughson and analysts Glenn Healy, Craig Simpson and Kelly Hrudey—would remain in place but now report to Rogers. At least Rogers would be paying the salaries of the broadcasters.

The changes resulted in a massive game of musical chairs for the CBC Sports staff, which was hit by dozens of layoffs. When the Rogers crew moved onto the eighth floor of the CBC building, home to *Hockey Night in Canada* as well as CBC Sports, producers and other executives, some with more than 30 years of service at the network, were kicked out of their offices. They were herded into a spot on the south side of the floor, crammed into desks among the remaining staff. But, one employee noted, more room opened up as more layoffs took effect.

"I'd say weird is a great way to put it," a *Hockey Night* staffer told *The Globe and Mail* about the scene on the eighth floor. Not long after the newcomers moved in, a notice went up that the eighth-floor boardroom was now off-limits to CBC staffers unless they received permission from Rogers.

The idea of kicking the CBC Sports people out of their offices and then stuffing them all together in one small area on the same floor with the Rogers people came from CBC Sports boss Jeffrey Orridge, according to one of the people involved with the move. When Rogers cut the CBC deal, Rogers Media president Keith Pelley and Sportsnet president Scott Moore told the CBC people they needed studio space in their building.

"The reason for that was there was no place we had. We knew we wanted to do something big," Moore said. "The alternative would have been buy a building, build a facility all in a year, which would have been a disaster."

Moore was given three options for the office and studio space. The one he selected was unused office space on the fifth floor but Orridge said no, they wanted the Rogers people on the eighth floor. Moore protested that he did not want to start kicking people out of their offices. Orridge insisted that was the way it had to be done.

"They knew they had to downsize the sports department so they wanted to go into a smaller space," Moore said. "It was hard, especially for me as the former head of CBC Sports, to come in and basically kick these people out of their offices. For the most part they were all really good about it. But it had to be really tough."

It certainly was. According to the aforementioned CBC staffer, the sense of weirdness was nothing compared to the anger all of them felt toward management in the wake of losing the rights.

"I'm angry at them. I'm angry at the CBC for how they handled this," the network employee said. "I think a lot of people are mad. They just fired 50 people in sports and those are people with families. This didn't have to happen."

What intensified the anger was the feeling by the employees that Orridge and the acting head of English-language services, Neil McEneaney, not only missed a chance to keep at least a smaller version of *Hockey Night in Canada* but they compounded the problem by making such a poor deal with Rogers in keeping the show on CBC's airwaves. The anger was also directed at CBC president Hubert Lacroix, blamed not only for the loss of NHL hockey and the resulting deal with Rogers but the layoffs, too.

"We get the call the NHL is going with Rogers and Rogers is in complete control and we have to negotiate with them," the CBC staffer said. "What do we do? We bend over and take what they demand.

"Nobody at CBC had the foresight to say, 'Okay you guys tell the entire country *Hockey Night* is off the air and by the way we know you need us because your channels can't be seen across the country.' Nobody had the guts to do that. We're sitting here next year with the deal, we get no revenue, all we have is the chance to promote our shows.

"The CBC is horribly, irreparably damaged and nobody had the balls to go in there and say [to Rogers] if you won't give us a better deal than that you're taking the heat."

Something else that angered the CBC's *Hockey Night* employees was that as the rights negotiations came down to the wire in late November 2013, management people were reassuring them that it looked like the CBC would keep the show. "They weren't dealing with reality at all," was one of the nicer things said by one of several employees.

Orridge insisted he and McEneaney made the best deal they could under the circumstances. Once the gatekeeper model and its five-billion-dollar bids entered the picture, the CBC simply did not have the money to stay in the fight, he said.

"In terms of access to the *Hockey Night* brand and access to the best in hockey, Canadian viewers are still going to be able to see that," Orridge said. "We're not trying to sound Pollyannaish about it but that is still the case. So all things being equal, this was the best possible outcome given the totality of the circumstances and because we have such a great working relationship with Rogers and we are in partnership with them on so many different levels."

Even though Pelley managed to bluff the CBC negotiators into making the one-sided deal, both he and Sportsnet president Scott Moore say Orridge and McEneaney were unfairly blamed for the result. There really wasn't much wiggle room for them, the Rogers duo said.

"What was their alternative?" Moore said. "They couldn't take the risk on [paying] the five billion dollars, they just couldn't. They were going to be out of it."

Someone with Bell Media agreed with Moore that the CBC simply was out of the game based on money. One thing Orridge and McEneaney could be faulted for, the Bell person said, was "they thought somehow the NHL was going to cut them a break because they're a 60-year partner with the CBC." And he thought they gave in too quickly to Pelley on the Rogers sub-licence deal. However, the Bell person also felt CBC president Hubert Lacroix should have been more involved and ordered his negotiators to pursue a partnership with Bell in the early days that might have saved the network a small piece of the pie.

Moore also said that the *Hockey Night* agreement saved a number of jobs among the CBC Sports staff, which went from 80-plus employees to around 35. If those employees were laid off, the CBC would have been on the hook for hundreds of thousands of dollars more in severance payments than what was already on the books because many of them were with the company for decades.

"What it did for the CBC was it kept all those technical people [employed] who otherwise they would have been laid off and would have incurred severance charges," Moore said. "One of the things people don't know about the CBC is that if we lay somebody off at Rogers, severance goes below the [bottom] line. It doesn't count toward your profits. At the CBC, they had no funding for severance and the government doesn't give you funding for severance so it comes straight out of your operating costs. It would have been a huge issue."

As it was, when the round of layoffs in the wake of the loss of the NHL rights was announced, the CBC's severance cost was $33.5 million.

It is hard to put an exact number on the job losses in the sports department because the employees were in several categories. There were regular employees, those under contract, which generally were the on-air broadcasters, and the freelance workers who made up the bulk of the *Hockey Night* production team. The latter two groups were not technically CBC employees, although the broadcasters were considered to be CBCers. The freelancers made up the largest group, which was most of the *Hockey Night* technical crew. In the television business, most of them worked on productions for Sportsnet, TSN and the CBC. It was not unusual for a sportswriter, for example, to run into a sound engineer at three games in a week and each time he was working for a different network.

Thus the entire crew on *Hockey Night* was usually more than 200 people per weekend but only around 20, by one staffer's estimate, were actually full-time CBC employees. Most of those 20 employees kept their jobs by switching to the Rogers version of *Hockey Night*. Some on-air people were not so fortunate.

Andi Petrillo, who was host of the iDesk segment of the show, was not retained by Rogers and went to the NHL Network. She came back to the CBC in 2015 as an Olympics host and in 2016 added the job of host of *Leafs Lunch* on TSN 1050 sports radio to her portfolio. Also out were play-by-play men Mark Lee and Steve Armitage, long-time CBCers who often appeared on games not involving the Maple Leafs. They were laid off by the network. Rogers wanted to keep Kevin Weekes, a panelist and analyst, but the former NHL goaltender opted to quit and take a job at the NHL Network.

Also lost was *Hockey Night*'s satellite radio show. It technically had a contract with SiriusXM Canada through the 2014–15 season, but the CBC always paid the production costs of about $400,000 a year. Despite the show's popularity, neither the CBC nor SiriusXM had much interest in covering those costs in the last year of the radio deal with the NHL (Rogers took over the radio rights for the 2015–16 season). The show went into limbo during talks between Rogers, the CBC and the satellite company, and it was officially cancelled in early October 2014 when a deal could not be reached. Moore thought about reviving the show in the fall of 2015 but it never came off.

The pain was felt by everyone at the network. In April 2014, Lacroix held a company-wide town hall meeting to tell the employees just what the impact was of losing the NHL rights. It was devastating.

Lacroix announced the CBC was expecting a $130-million shortfall in revenue just for the 2014–15 broadcast year, on top of the $115-million cut dealt by the federal government two years earlier. Most of the shortfall was attributed to the loss of advertising from *Hockey Night*, although the CBC was also dealing with an overall softening of the advertising market just like other networks.

The CBC would also have to deal with advertising losses in the future for other shows that were due to the loss of the hockey rights. CBC's sales staff would no longer be able to tell advertisers that if they wanted time on the highest-rated show on the network they would also have to buy time on other less popular shows.

"The one thing they don't get is what we call the halo effect," Moore said. "If you go to Honda and sell them a big sponsorship on *Hockey Night*, they're also buying *The Rick Mercer Report*."

The round of layoffs announced by Lacroix was the third for the CBC since 2009. This time, 657 jobs were eliminated. This brought the total number of lost jobs to about 2,100 in five years. The 657 jobs lost in 2014 represented 8 per cent of the network's 8,000 employees in both the CBC's English-language division and Radio-Canada, the French-language service. Some of the job losses were dealt with by attrition or not filling vacant positions or moving people to different departments, but the vast majority of them were employees who were pushed out the door.

Lacroix also announced there would be cuts to programming across the board and the CBC would no longer bid on professional sports properties. Its biggest sports events are now the Olympics, which the CBC has until 2024. The Games became affordable for the CBC when both Rogers and Bell, soured by their experiment in working together as a consortium for the 2010 and 2012 Olympics, declined to bid again for the Games. However, both companies agreed to become partners with the CBC in the same arrangement as the NHL deal between Rogers and CBC, carrying events with the advertising dollars going to the CBC.

After the NHL rights were lost, the first big athletics event the CBC carried was the 2014 Winter Olympics in Sochi, Russia. That seemed to go smoothly enough, although the network's coverage budget was in place before the surprise announcement that it had lost the NHL rights.

Trouble struck at the Pan American Games in July 2015 in Toronto when the CBC missed live conventional television coverage of both the men's baseball gold-medal game between Canada and the US and the women's basketball gold-medal game between Canada and the US. Neither game was shown live on regular television but both were streamed live online. However, the quality of the Internet stream was inconsistent and the audiences were far smaller than those for the television events.

The CBC told the *National Post* it was getting audiences as large as one million for Pan Am events on conventional television. But the network planned to show most of the games online—about 650 hours of streaming according to the CBC's initial planning—with just five hours per day set for television. When it turned out there was more demand for the Pan Ams than expected, the CBC increased its television hours but not enough to avoid controversy.

The online audience for the men's baseball game was 57,780, the network told the *National Post*, while 44,818 saw the women's basketball game. Canada won both games and there was lots of bellyaching on social media about the CBC's faux pas. If the games had been on conventional television they could have easily attracted 500,000 or more viewers.

"We certainly recognize you're never going to make everyone happy," Chuck Thompson, head of public affairs, CBC English services, told the *National Post*. "For sure, resources are a factor in what we've been able to provide. But our commitment to amateur sport is as strong as ever."

But the CBC went on to a spectacular success at the 2016 Summer Olympics in Rio de Janeiro with record-breaking television ratings, although the CBC threw more resources at that event than the Pan Am Games, which are minor-league by comparison. The largest television audience for a Summer Olympics in Canadian history, 7.2 million, watched Canadian Andre De Grasse lose to Usain Bolt in the men's 200-metre sprint. When Bolt won the men's 100 metres over De Grasse, 5.3 million Canadians tuned in. Between the CBC and French-language Radio-Canada, 32.1 million people watched at some point, which represented 9 in 10 Canadians. It was a much-needed success for the CBC, which has now settled into its niche as the go-to network for Olympic-style sports.

The network certainly signalled this niche was its plan for the future when it hired Greg Stremlaw in the fall of 2015 to replace Jeffrey Orridge as the head of CBC Sports. Stremlaw was not a television executive, having spent most of his career running various sports organizations. He came to the CBC from Curling Canada. The network wanted Stremlaw because of his relationships with the sports federations not only in the Olympic world but in other sports outside the mainstream.

Shortly after he was hired, Stremlaw told *The Globe and Mail* he planned to continue forming partnerships with Bell and Rogers for the big-ticket events like the Olympics and go it alone in the lower-profile sports.

"I believe these partnerships are a great way for us to maximize CBC Sports's expertise and bring that nation-building experience to all Canadians in a financially prudent manner," Stremlaw said.

Orridge left the CBC to become the commissioner of the Canadian Football League. This is not a job for the faint of heart, given the league's aging audience and, most of all, the strange mix of community and private ownership among the nine teams, all with their own agendas. His time in the job was spent lurching from one crisis to another and by June 2017, Orridge was gone after 25 months. It was by "mutual agreement" as the saying goes.

McEneaney also left the CBC in the wake of the loss of the NHL rights. He wound up as president of Numeris, the primary provider of television and radio ratings in Canada. The company has its critics in the broadcast industry but McEneaney's perch is far safer than being commissioner of the CFL.

While CBC Sports grappled with its new reality, there was a celebratory mood down the hall as the Rogers version of *Hockey Night in Canada* plus the rest of the hockey broadcasts got down to work. Actually, reworking the broadcasts began months before the Rogers troops moved into the CBC building. Before Pelley and Moore even came to a rights agreement with Bettman, Collins and Daly, they were also discussing who they would like to see on the broadcasts. The first big name to come up was TSN's James Duthie.

Ron MacLean, the long-time *Hockey Night* host, probably never had a chance to keep the job he held since March 1987 when he replaced Dave Hodge. The latter was fired by the CBC after he made his displeasure plain on the air over a network executive's decision not to switch the broadcast to a Montreal–Philadelphia game in overtime when a Maple Leafs–Flames game ended early. MacLean's testy relationship with Bettman plus the eagerness of Pelley and Moore to put a Rogers stamp on the show meant the holdover host was unlikely to remain as the Saturday night host.

It was clear from the start Rogers' relationship with the NHL was going to be a partnership. Aside from comments by Pelley and Moore to that effect, one of Bettman's jokes at the big press conference to announce the deal made it clear the league was going to have a lot of influence on the hockey broadcasts.

As the press conference on November 26, 2013, was nearing the end, Rogers broadcaster Daren Millard, destined to be a midweek host in the new lineup, made a mild joke about how there were struggling franchises in the US. Next to him on the stage, Bettman responded with, "You now have to play nice," which drew a laugh from the audience. When Millard said that would take some getting used to, Bettman said, "Well you'd better get used to it quick."

It was not said entirely in a humorous vein. Bettman knew the entire roster of Rogers broadcasters was in the room. A message was delivered. Since the audience was almost entirely made up of journalists, the next question was just how much leeway would Sportsnet people have to question the NHL considering the enormous financial bond between Rogers and the NHL. "The number-one thing is maintaining journalistic integrity," Pelley said. Bettman decided to back off a bit, saying, "we would insist on nothing less. Our fans want authenticity. We never control the coverage of our game—which is obvious by some of the treatment." It was easy to see a jab at the CBC in Bettman's last sentence.

Thus it was little surprise the first serious contender to replace MacLean as host was Duthie. He would have been the first choice of a lot of broadcasting executives and a lot of hockey fans. By late 2013, Duthie had been the host of TSN's hockey broadcasts for more than 10 years and he also served as one of the hosts for the 2010 and 2012 Olympics, with multiple Gemini awards to his credit. Duthie was 47 at the time, just six years younger than MacLean, but he was perceived as a young, hip broadcaster, mostly because of his quick-witted sense of humour.

Almost as soon as the switch in NHL rights was announced, Pelley and Moore made it known to Duthie they had him in mind for the host's job. Duthie was also made aware that money was not a problem. Despite the tempting overture, Duthie politely declined because of his strong loyalty to TSN, which hired the Ottawa native in 1998 and moved him up the ladder to become the anchor of its hockey broadcasts. By the time Rogers approached him, Duthie was regarded within the industry as the best sports television host in Canada.

He never talked about his chance to be the face of *Hockey Night in Canada* other than to acknowledge he had the opportunity. "All that matters is that I will be staying at TSN," he wrote in an email to *The Globe and Mail*. Similar answers were given to other reporters.

Phil King, then president of CTV and sports programming for Bell Media, and TSN president Stewart Johnston moved quickly to lock up their key hockey talent and boost morale at the network. Bob McKenzie, Ray Ferraro, Darren Dreger, Pierre LeBrun and several others along with Duthie were all given new contracts with healthy raises. Duthie scored a four-year deal reportedly worth $1 million per year and was promised a wider range of hosting duties like the Grey Cup, soccer's World Cup and the Masters golf tournament.

Fending off Rogers' pursuit of Duthie and the pre-emptive strike of signing up McKenzie and the other hockey guys did much to shore up morale at TSN in the weeks after the loss of the NHL rights. Management announced the signings all at once to the staff in the TSN newsroom in an obvious move to boost employees' spirits.

It was a significant victory for TSN and could not have been managed if all of the broadcasters had not had a strong loyalty to the company. The McKenzie and Ferraro contracts were also significant because each is considered the best at his specialty. McKenzie is the man who pioneered the role of NHL insider who breaks most of the news around the league and Ferraro is arguably the best game analyst, a more subjective judgement to be sure.

"Duthie was a big one because that sent a pretty strong message to TSN [employees]. If he's staying, things are pretty good," McKenzie said.

TSN only lost two on-air people to Rogers, CFL host Dave Randorf and hockey analyst Mike Johnson. Randorf was hired as one of Rogers' four play-by-play broadcasters, the other three being Jim Hughson and Bob Cole, both *Hockey Night* veterans, and Paul Romanuk. Johnson became the game analyst on the second Rogers team, working mainly with Romanuk.

There were a couple of losses for TSN in the executive suite. Gord Cutler was not technically a TSN employee when he was hired by Scott Moore to be in charge of all Rogers' hockey broadcasts with the title of senior vice-president of NHL production. His most recent job before that was executive producer for Canada's Olympic Broadcast Media Consortium. Cutler produced the prime-time broadcasts for both the 2010 and 2012 Olympics, so he was working for Bell Media in part. But Cutler spent much of his early career working for TSN, which is where he learned his trade as a hockey producer. Mitch Kerzner was a veteran TSN producer who was hired by Moore to be senior executive producer, studio, which meant he had a voice in operating *Hockey Night* but was also responsible for assembling and running the various panels on each of the hockey shows.

After the rights were lost there was some angst among the broadcast staff at TSN but they quickly adopted the attitude McKenzie showed just after he got the scoop that TSN and the CBC lost the NHL rights to Rogers. "We've got a boatload of gifted, hard-working people at TSN who are up for the challenge of keeping TSN as THE source for all things hockey," McKenzie tweeted shortly before Rogers and the NHL made the official announcement.

In part, at least, McKenzie's defiant tweet became true. Rogers may have had the national games three and sometimes four nights a week but TSN remained the go-to network in a news sense. TSN remained the ratings leader by a wide margin over Sportsnet for the two non-game NHL shows where they go head-to-head against each other, the NHL trade deadline day in late February and free-agent day every July 1. The panel shows also did well in the ensuing seasons, as they ran with the regional games TSN still had, led by 26 Toronto Maple Leafs games.

TSN also scored one advertising coup over Sportsnet in Rogers' first season of the new deal. Tim Hortons, always a major hockey advertiser, decided not to become a title sponsor with any of the Rogers hockey broadcasts. A title sponsorship is a lucrative deal for networks because the advertiser pays extra to have its name on the show title as well as for the regular spots. In this case, TSN's panel, interview and highlights show *That's Hockey* was rechristened *Tim Hortons That's Hockey* for the start of the 2014–15 NHL season.

There were still hockey games to be seen on TSN. The network still had the regional rights to the Winnipeg Jets, it had 26 Leafs games in splitting their regional package with Rogers starting in 2014–15, and it outbid Rogers handily to get the Ottawa Senators' English and French rights for both television and radio. Plus there was the world junior championship, an event TSN made its own over the years.

The Senators' rights package was for 12 years and as much as $400 million for a minimum of 52 games per year in English and 40 in French. That works out to an average of $33.3 million per year for 12 years, which was a lifeline for Senators owner Eugene Melnyk, who was hit by a series of financial reverses at that time. The attraction for TSN was that Ottawa shared the same regional market with the Montreal Canadiens—a slice of Eastern Ontario, Québec and Atlantic Canada. The interesting thing here was that when Bell Media matched TVA Sports' bid for the Montreal Canadiens' French-language regional rights it decided to cede the English regional rights to Rogers at the same time, probably because the Habs' English market was much smaller than the French one, which wound up costing $60 million per year thanks to TVA. However, TSN got the Habs' English regional rights back for the 2017–18 season, outbidding Rogers.

The powers at Bell Media decided it was time for a makeover after losing the national NHL games to Rogers. TSN added three new channels to TSN1 and TSN2, naming them all numerically up to TSN5. The network had lots of programming, often more than it could air at once when there were only two feeds. The three new feeds allowed TSN to show more games from the properties it had from its association with ESPN like NCAA football, for example, and more from the soccer World Cup.

The network decided on what came to be called the "championship approach," emphasizing its properties with a lot of major championships outside of hockey. This included the NFL and the Super Bowl, the Grey Cup, all four tennis Grand Slam tournaments, the Masters in golf and both the men's and women's World Cup in soccer from 2015 through 2026.

By the end of 2015, TSN president Stewart Johnston said he and his fellow Bell Media executives were happy with the way the network weathered the storm, even if Rogers was celebrating its ascension to No. 1 among Canada's sports networks, based on its average monthly ratings over the year.

"We were long-time partners with the NHL and, yes, we were very disappointed," Johnston said. "We certainly saw externally some question marks about the future of our network. We were going to regroup and determine what was the right direction for us to go. That direction was the five-feed strategy which was created to drive value for our subscribers.

"We knew we had an incredible amount of really high value content, enough to feed five feeds, offer choice for the consumer. That was the starting point for the strategy and it really knocked into place in the year that was just reported on. I think we're very pleased to see the results of that strategy."

TSN was always the most profitable network in comparison to Sportsnet and that, too, changed as TSN lost its grip on the top spot in the ratings. According to the CRTC, TSN had a pre-tax profit of $84.7 million in 2016, down from $103.5 million in 2014. TSN had 8.5 million subscribers in 2016, a drop of 500,000 from just over 9 million in 2014. Sportsnet turned a profit of $43.7 million in

2014 and it rose to $93.6 million in 2016. Sportsnet had 8.1 million subscribers in 2016, down slightly from 8.3 million in 2014.

Bell Media executives like to say they thank their lucky stars they don't have to pay $5.2 billion to the NHL in light of the trouble Rogers had in the first two years of the contract. But their own programming costs climbed steeply in the same period thanks to the overall trend of rising fees for sports properties. In 2013, according to CRTC figures, TSN paid $62.6 million in rights fees, a drop of $34.2 million from the previous year, although it is not clear if that represents the loss of the NHL national rights. But by 2016, TSN paid $127.5 million in rights fees, more than double what was paid in 2013.

In the same three-year period, Sportsnet's rights costs went from $83.9 million to $263 million, which definitely reflects the cost of the NHL deal. However, broadcast executives from both Rogers and Bell say that $263 million—which is actually the total of all programming rights not just hockey—does not reflect what was actually paid to the NHL. They say that in a company's financial statements, the money paid to the NHL is spread around to different networks and divisions in Rogers Media to ease the impact. Any subsidiary that has anything to do with the NHL is eligible to be assessed part of the cost.

Keith Pelley is well aware of his rivals' chuckling about Rogers' annual obligation to the NHL and has a ready response: "I always laughed at the guys at Bell who said we overpaid. I went, 'Hmmm, you guys were going to pay the same and yet we also have the [TVA Sports] deal that is going to mitigate our risk.' I'm pretty comfortable with this contract now."

Over at Rogers, the spring and summer of 2014 were a happy series of seminars to show the hockey employees what was planned for the new version of *Hockey Night in Canada* and the other national broadcasts, press events to introduce the new and hold-over broadcasters as well as some high-tech features for the shows and splashy presentations to potential advertisers. The crowning event was a three-day seminar at the tony Shangri-La Hotel in downtown Toronto for the hockey staff. It was capped by a big party at the equally exclusive Ritz-Carlton. Times were good.

But first there was a little unpleasantness to be dealt with. Few people in the industry were surprised when the news about Rogers' pursuit of James Duthie confirmed Ron MacLean was out as host of *Hockey Night*. But it did come as a shock to millions of television viewers even if the folksy, pun-loving MacLean was not everyone's cup of tea.

While there is no doubt Pelley and Moore wanted to put their own stamp on *Hockey Night*, the majority opinion of broadcast insiders was that NHL commissioner Gary Bettman wielded considerable sway over MacLean's demotion. Not that anyone would say so but this is one of those instances where the relationship between Bettman and MacLean was so bad no one had to spell anything out. Certainly MacLean was willing to consider the possibility.

He told *The Globe and Mail* that pressure from the top levels of the NHL to tone down any criticism was nothing new. The CBC was often the focus of unhappiness in the commissioner's office when MacLean or someone else would let loose on Bettman or the league.

"I did my best to sort of walk about," MacLean said. "I don't want to be a complete gunslinger or maverick. But I felt strongly about the importance of a healthy players' association. That was a difficult thing for both the CBC and the league to accept, always was."

MacLean said he was surprised when the bad news was delivered but deep down he knew the possibility of being replaced was always there. He was aware of not only Bettman's ire but also that of the owners, who often accused MacLean of being biased toward the players on labour issues.

"I was caught obviously a little flatfooted and yet I wasn't because Scott [Moore] always said that is the challenge, working with the league is very important to us," MacLean said. "The owners weren't happy about that particular thing and maybe that hurt me but I would gladly fall on my sword for that principle. But I don't know that it had anything to do with this. It could have. I've always known John Collins is very conscious about polishing the shield of the NHL brand. That kind of thing might have hurt me but it wasn't something I was ever going to worry about."

MacLean admitted his persistence in advancing the players' cause "was a bit of an anchor in my career." But he never considered changing. "My hero was [writer] Lewis Lapham and his basic point was always one I lived by—I'm not going to trade in the ability to think for myself for a five-star hotel or a nice job where everybody knows your name. That just couldn't happen."

Once the 2014–15 season started, MacLean would only serve as Don Cherry's sidekick on *Coach's Corner* on *Hockey Night*. He would remain with Rogers as a host but it would be for the new *Rogers Hometown Hockey* show on Sunday nights. MacLean was to work on Sundays with co-host Tara Slone, a rock singer who was also co-host of *Breakfast Television* on City in Calgary.

MacLean and Slone were to be the on-location hosts on Sunday nights. They would travel to a different Canadian city or town and introduce stories from local rinks or other establishments with lots of interaction with the citizens of those communities. Rogers looked on it as a community-relations exercise and publicity and marketing venture for its cable, satellite and wireless services. In that sense, MacLean was the perfect choice as the face of the show since he always liked interactions with the fans. MacLean also came out of the shakeup with a new four-year contract, so it wasn't as if anyone was looking for him to quit.

Pelley and Moore made an unconventional choice for MacLean's replacement to say the least. Once again the CBC was poached, but this time it was the entertainment department that was robbed. George Stroumboulopoulos, a long-time host of pop-culture talk shows at the CBC, was the next pick to be the host of *Hockey Night in Canada* after Duthie decided to stay with TSN.

Moore was familiar with Stroumboulopoulos from his days running CBC Sports. After getting his start with Toronto sports radio station The Fan 590 in 1993, Stroumboulopoulos was a MuchMusic producer and host in the early 2000s. He wound up full-time at the CBC in 2005 when he was hired to be host of *The Hour*, an interview and feature show that mixed politics, pop culture, entertainment and other topics. It quickly became popular and the name of the show was changed to *George Stroumboulopoulos Tonight*. Stroumboulopoulos was now *the* hip young star of the stodgy old CBC.

Moore, who was impressed by Stroumboulopoulos's interviewing skills, thought he would be the right look for a show that was going to transform from the comfortable old sweater Canadians wore for generations to a younger, state-of-the-art show with all of the requisite bells and whistles. Stroumboulopoulos was 42 when his first season as host began in 2014, 12 years younger than MacLean, and he had the pierced ear, soul patch and skinny suits to go with the new hip look of the show.

When he was introduced at a press conference, Stroumboulopoulos deferred to MacLean and did not have a lot to say. Then again, most of the questions concerned his age—even though at 42 Stroumboulopoulos was 15 years older than MacLean was when he became host in 1987—and his wardrobe plans for the show, so at times Stroumboulopoulos appeared nonplussed. "I think I'm the oldest guy to ever get this position," he said at one point and, "I'm just happy to be a part of this team."

In addition to Stroumboulopoulos, the *Hockey Night* show kept Elliotte Friedman and Kelly Hrudey from the CBC version as well as *Coach's Corner* with MacLean and Don Cherry. Scott Oake also came along as the pre- and post-game interviewer along with Friedman. Hrudey once again did the panels with *Hockey Night* newcomer Nick Kypreos, a Sportsnet veteran. Also appearing on the panels were Friedman and Damien Cox, who gave up his regular sports column at the *Toronto Star* to expand his moonlighting role at Rogers. Cox and Friedman also did a news segment discussing the top hockey stories of the week. Reporter Cassie Campbell-Pascall and analysts Gary Galley, Greg Millen and P.J. Stock came over too, although Stock had a less prominent role.

The number-one broadcast crew for Hockey Night was play-by-play man Jim Hughson with Craig Simpson and Glenn Healy. Analyst Mike Johnson usually worked with Paul Romanuk while Millen and broadcasting legend Bob Cole were the third pairing. Cole, who made no secret of the fact he was not happy the CBC gave his spot on the top team to Hughson a few years earlier, was thrilled Rogers wanted him to keep working.

"It's a little shot in the arm," said Cole, who turned 81 the summer Rogers took over. "It's pretty nice when they look at your work and say, 'He hasn't screwed up much, he sounds okay.' I'd go nuts, I really would, if someone all of a sudden said you're not doing it."

Unfortunately for Cole, the day someone said you're not doing it came faster than he expected. While he was not on Rogers' No. 1 broadcast team, Cole still called games deep into the playoffs, through the NHL's conference finals. But in the 2017 playoffs Cole only called games in the first two rounds and during the 2017–18 regular season Cole's workload was cut back by the Sportsnet bosses.

The big shock came in the 2018 playoffs when Cole was benched for the duration. He was replaced by Rick Ball, who called Calgary Flames games for Sportsnet and is considered a rising star. It was the first time in five decades Cole was not broadcasting NHL playoff games. It caught him by surprise and he made his feelings clear in an exclusive story from the *National Post*.

"The decision sure wasn't mutual," Cole told Post hockey columnist Michael Traikos. "It was right out of the blue. Rogers decided to go with other [broadcast] teams and I have to live with that. But it was their decision—not mine."

Network insiders said there was not a lot said internally about the decision to ground Cole but the impression was given upper management decided it was time to give an up-and-comer like Ball more important games.

However, the decision was not a complete surprise. Cole's work was the subject of debate for several years with critics, both in the mainstream media and fans on social media, calling into question the broadcaster's ability to recognize players and keep up with the play. But Cole long resisted any suggestion he should slow down let alone retire. He is the kind of guy who thought baseball broadcasting legend Vin Scully took early retirement when he finally stepped down in 2016 at the age of 89.

The decision by Rogers immediately called into question Cole's future with the company. While he told Traikos he was not ready to retire, Cole also said he did not know if he would be calling 2018–19 regular-season games.

While Rogers missed out on landing Tim Hortons and Canadian Tire as title sponsors, it did sign up one of the big four Canadian banks to put its name on the Wednesday broadcasts plus the annual *Hockey Day in Canada*. *Scotiabank Wednesday Night Hockey* would have Sportsnet veteran Daren Millard as the host. Jeff Marek, who used to work on *Hockey Night* before going to Sportsnet in 2011, was tapped to host Thursday games plus the Saturday afternoon edition of *Hockey Central Saturday*, the pre-game show.

The new and old faces of the Rogers version of *Hockey Night* were introduced by Scott Moore at a splashy press conference in the Glenn Gould Theatre at CBC's headquarters. The irony of seeing the victors of the NHL rights battle celebrated on the loser's stage did not go unnoticed by at least some CBC staffers.

"Don't screw this up, it's a big show," was the opening comment from Ron MacLean to George Stroumboulopoulos when they were introduced by Moore. There were lots of ways to take the admonition, from a wry don't fumble the biggest opportunity in Canadian sports broadcasting to don't alienate the powers that be like I did.

There was an omen of what would come to dog Stroumbou-lopoulos during his run as host in all those questions from the media about what he planned to wear and if the viewers would accept someone with an earring. Stroumboulopoulos professed he "hadn't thought about it" and as for the earring, he said the fans would probably tune in for the hockey, not to check out what he was sporting in jewelry. Unfortunately for him, that turned out not to be the case, especially when the poor performances of the Canadian teams resulted in a large group of viewers angrily looking for something to complain about.

But in the spring of 2014, the unhappiness of viewers was barely even a passing thought. The people in the hockey depart-ment at Rogers were living charmed lives as the darlings of the company who were given all the resources they needed. The budget and job cuts that were starting to take hold elsewhere in Rogers and over at Bell as a result of cord-cutting did not apply to the hockey productions.

After all, come October 2014 there were going to be more games on more networks than Canadians had ever seen. Rogers planned to deliver 533 regular-season games on 13 networks plus digital platforms and, in the spring, every single NHL playoff game. This will not be your father's *Hockey Night in Canada* seemed to be the theme.

Rogers did keep Toronto filmmaker Tim Thompson on *Hockey Night*'s staff. He was responsible for the popular musical montages incorporating hockey highlights that opened the CBC version of the show. Moore said the montages would still be used, only not as much. More money would be spent on animated openings with what was called a "video-game" look. The marriage between Thompson and Rogers was not a happy one, as the musical openings disappeared quickly. Thompson left the show by the end of the first season.

The crown jewel of the new shows was the $4.5-million studio Rogers built in the CBC's broadcast centre. It was to be used for every NHL broadcast and was dominated by a video monitor called Goliath that was 12 metres (38 feet) wide and 3.4 metres (11 feet) high. There were 14 cameras and nine sets, including the central desk and an interview area for Stroumboulopoulos that featured armchairs rather than the traditional desk. A glass floor allowed for the markings of a virtual rink to be projected on it, which allowed analysts to break down plays by using hockey sticks rather than pointers.

Rogers kept its promise to Bettman and Collins about promoting the NHL across all of its platforms and even on non-sports ones. As the 2014–15 season approached, advertising for the hockey broadcasts went across most of its properties. The Shopping Channel was pushing NHL merchandise and there were cringe-worthy segments on shows like *Breakfast Television* where hosts tried on team sweaters and directed viewers to the Shopping Channel. Feature stories on hockey appeared in *Today's Parent* magazine and even crept into the women's magazine *Chatelaine*.

All Rogers systems were go.

9

A TURBULENT MAIDEN VOYAGE

Due to the turbulence of Rogers' first two seasons in charge of the national NHL hockey broadcasts this is often forgotten, but at the start of their first season the optimism around Toronto among hockey fans was understandable. The Maple Leafs, the team that drove the ratings more than any other, were finally showing signs of life. People were excited about their chances and by extension so were the Rogers executives.

The Maple Leafs surprised everyone when they made the playoffs for the first time in seven years by running up a 26-17-5 record in the lockout-shortened 2012–13 season. They finished fifth in the Eastern Conference and played the fourth-place Boston Bruins in the first round. The Bruins, who won the Stanley Cup in 2011, were the overwhelming favourite, in no small part because they always managed to smother the Leafs' best player, ex-Bruin Phil Kessel.

But the Leafs managed to take the best-of-seven series to the limit with Kessel playing a central role. Then in Game 7 at the TD Garden in Boston, the Leafs shocked just about everyone around the NHL by taking a 4-1 lead into the third period. The roof fell in when the youthful Leafs suddenly realized what they were about to do and swallowed hard. When the Bruins scored early in the third period there was a sense of the inevitable. The Bruins scored twice in the last two minutes to force overtime. Their fans, backed by Bon Jovi's "Living on a Prayer" cranked to full volume, created an intimidating wall of sound that did not let up for the entire 17-minute intermission and through overtime until the Bruins won it six minutes and five seconds in on a goal by Patrice Bergeron. It was the first time an NHL team came back to win Game 7 of a playoff series after being down three goals in the third period.

There was some of the expected grousing in the media and among the fans about the Leafs blowing such a big lead. But since the team's better players were still in their early and mid-20s it did not last long. There was a sense that with players like Kessel, Jake Gardiner, James van Riemsdyk, Nazem Kadri and even the often-beleaguered captain Dion Phaneuf, general manager Brian Burke's rebuilding plan was about to pay off in the season following the loss to the Bruins. Not that Burke was around to see it. He was fired on the eve of the previous season and replaced by his top assistant, Dave Nonis.

It was with thoughts of the rising Leafs in mind, along with the Montreal Canadiens, who finished second in the Eastern Conference in 2012–13 and had the best goaltender in the world in Carey Price, and the Vancouver Canucks, third in the Western Conference, that Rogers executives projected a 20-per-cent jump in the television ratings in the first season. In the seven years leading up to Rogers' first season, the CBC's ratings for the first game on *Hockey Night* stayed around two million viewers with one million staying to watch the late game. Up until 2013 those were all years the Leafs missed the playoffs, so the predictions of more viewers made sense.

Rogers revamped its advertising sales department well ahead of the season to be in position to capitalize on the hockey deal. Jack Tomik was hired away from the CBC in May 2013 to run the sales department and direct its change in approach. Tomik's job was to move the group from the old method, where sales people handled just one form of advertising, such as radio, to the new system of allowing a client to buy ads on all platforms from one person. But the changes did not come without bruises.

Under Tomik's restructuring, at least four senior executives in sales left the company in 2014. Tomik himself departed in November 2014, which raised eyebrows throughout the industry. While movement is common in ad sales, industry sources thought Tomik's mandate was for at least three years and he left 19 months into it. While there was conjecture Tomik's departure was not his idea, no one at Rogers wanted to discuss it in detail. Al Dark, another CBC veteran, replaced Tomik.

"Dealing with an overall restructuring of the company, he just wasn't having as much fun as he'd like to," Sportsnet president Scott Moore told *The Globe and Mail*. Tomik himself did not respond to a request for comment.

With the optimistic audience projections adding to the pressure of raising enough revenue to pay the high cost of the rights, the Rogers sales people were firm with prospective buyers. The ad rates were also raised to reflect the expected 20-per-cent jump in viewers. This is where Rogers met resistance for the first time.

"In my estimation, I think Rogers was very aggressive in their estimate for how much hockey Canadians are interested in seeing and how much that's worth to advertisers," Fred Forster, the chief executive officer of Omnicom Media Group Canada, a major media buyer, told *The Globe and Mail*.

Price was said to be the reason both Tim Hortons and Canadian Tire did not buy a title sponsorship for one of the national hockey broadcasts. No one from Tim Hortons would comment. A source close to senior management at Canadian Tire told *The Globe and Mail* that was exactly why the retail giant pulled back.

"At the right price we would have been in," the source said. "We had nothing against Rogers or the deal. However for us, we only have so many marketing dollars we want to spend overall and we look for the highest return.

"I think they know we're always open to talking but we want to see how it settles out. We'll just wait until it's the right price for what we're getting."

Both Tim Hortons and Canadian Tire wound up buying individual spots on Rogers hockey games but at modest levels. Like Forster, the Canadian Tire source also wondered if Rogers guessed wrong on Canadians' appetite for hockey. There would be more games televised than ever before and *Rogers Hometown Hockey* added a whole new night to the mix, a show that would have to compete with NFL football and more competitive regular prime-time viewing than Saturday nights, both deeply entrenched habits for viewers. This thought occurred to people at Rogers, too. "It's a lot of freakin' hockey," one executive told *The Globe and Mail*.

The resistance of advertisers did not come as a surprise to old CBC hands. One veteran staffer said that in its last season of 2013–14, the network could not get a title sponsor for its pre-game show, and one for the three stars of the game was not found until the start of the playoffs. The 2014 Olympics was partly to blame for this, the CBC person said, as advertisers did not have budgets big enough to buy time on both, but it was still part of a troubling trend that started a few years earlier.

However, Rogers executives were not pulling these projections out of the air. In the months leading up to the season, they spent a lot of time and money surveying people across Canada about what they wanted to see in the Rogers versions of the hockey broadcasts.

What Rogers called a "listening tour" was put together in February 2014 with representatives from both Rogers and the NHL. The group went to all seven NHL cities in Canada plus three smaller cities where hockey interest was judged to be especially strong—Red Deer, Alberta; Sudbury, Ontario; and Kingston, Ontario. The plan was to talk to people connected with the local minor hockey associations, go into sports pubs and even homes to gather information.

Rogers wanted to find out how to reach younger fans and how to reach them aside from just the game being on conventional television. With millennials watching more TV online and often watching a second screen like an iPad or mobile phone, Rogers wanted to find out what it should emphasize in its social-media approach to games and which digital channels young viewers were watching. The major result from the tour and other research reassured Rogers executives they were on the right track.

"It came back through the research that people wanted more games on more platforms and that's what we're doing," Rogers Media president Keith Pelley told *The Globe and Mail*.

When it came to the broadcasts, Rogers combined the fancy new touches it wanted, from the high-tech studio where new host George Stroumboulopoulos would stand rather than sit at a desk, with the most popular holdovers from the CBC's version of the show. The most popular of all, of course, was *Coach's Corner*. Don Cherry's hold on the attention of Canada's hockey fans was still such that his segment made the transition essentially untouched, at least in form. Which was just fine with the crusty octogenarian, whose concern with the state of *Hockey Night in Canada* began and ended with his segment.

"I knew that Rogers would never mess with the greatest segment on television," Cherry was quoted as saying in a Sportsnet press release. At the press conference to introduce the new version of the show Cherry said, "I know one thing. They won't fool with

Coach's Corner. And that's the main thing, isn't it?" He also told reporters he signed a new contract with Rogers for two years. But not fooling with *Coach's Corner* wasn't going to last long.

Another holdover from the CBC but much newer than *Coach's Corner* also made the jump to Rogers. The Punjabi broadcasts, introduced by the CBC because Punjabi was the third-most spoken language in Canada behind English and French, moved to Rogers' Omni Television. Play-by-play announcer Harnarayan Singh would become a social-media phenomenon in June 2016 when his "Bonino, Bonino, Bonino, Bonino" call of Pittsburgh Penguins centre Nick Bonino's game-winning goal against the San Jose Sharks in the first game of the Stanley Cup final went viral.

Rogers also introduced *Hockey 101*, a series of video shorts that explained the jargon and rules of hockey for new Canadians. They made their debut in eight languages with plans to add six more languages and were shown on Sportsnet's web site, Omni, Rogers' multi-language station and online. "I think it's a huge untapped market," Moore told *The Globe and Mail*. "It's a very multicultural country and we're now competing with basketball and soccer. We need to be able to bring those viewers in."

There was a play for both new Canadians and young viewers with Rogers streaming all the games it broadcast to all types of mobile devices. Researcher Gord Hendren, president of Charlton Insights in Toronto, told *The Globe and Mail* new Canadians have the same love for mobile technology—tablets, smartphones and laptops—as young people.

When Rogers' first season with the NHL rights began, Charlton's research found conventional television was still the most popular platform with 95 per cent of NHL viewers. But most of them now watch with at least two screens. Plus, 62 per cent of the viewers used a computer to watch the NHL in the 2012–13 season and 30 per cent watched on a mobile device. The research company also found the number of fans who follow the league on Facebook went from 34 per cent in the 2010–11 season to 47 per cent by 2012–13. Hendren said those numbers would keep growing.

The pace of change was also speeding up at *Hockey Night*. The holdover staff from the CBC was buffeted not only by seeing the show come under Rogers' control but by an influx of new production staff from both Rogers and TSN. This was disquieting for some but for others like analyst Glenn Healy, who worked between the benches on the number-one team, it was like putting together an all-star team.

"Looking at some of the guys they brought over from some of the networks you're not getting a better truck than that anywhere in the world," Healy said, referring to the trucks outside the arenas that house the producers and directors and other technical staff. "For me it's total satisfaction."

With senior vice-president, NHL production, Gord Cutler now in charge of all Rogers hockey broadcasts, the *Hockey Night* staff was due for more culture shock. Maybe cultural whiplash is a better phrase. Not only was Rogers now putting its stamp on their show, someone from TSN also had a big say in matters. Cutler cut his hockey production teeth at TSN, where they were not fans of the CBC's more conservative approach to hockey broadcasting.

When TSN launched in 1984 it was the first time in many years the CBC had a direct Canadian rival as a hockey broadcaster. By then the CBC was secure in its reputation as the gold standard for producing hockey games anywhere in the world. As the new kid on the block, TSN liked to tweak the nose of its older competitor and it wasn't long before there was real animosity between the employees of each company. However, this was all done behind the scenes rather than on the air, so the tension remained below the surface.

Cutler was careful not to say anything publicly about his thoughts on how the CBC produced hockey games in the months leading up to the launch of the Rogers version of *Hockey Night*. But there was no shortage of CBC holdover employees on the show and ex-CBCers who would say, anonymously of course, they could sense Cutler's dislike of the CBC way of doing things.

Before Rogers took over, Joel Darling and Steve Sloan were the co-executive producers of *Hockey Night*. But neither one made it to the starting line with the show. Darling, who had a long connection with *Hockey Night*, remained a CBC employee but was placed in charge of producing the NHL's special events for Rogers, such as the all-star game and outdoor games. Sloan was not kept on by Rogers.

The clash of cultures came to a head early in the season with someone who was no stranger to butting heads with management—Don Cherry. With the CBC, Cherry and MacLean grew used to stretching their time on *Coach's Corner* during the first intermission. By the last of the CBC years, the segment would often go well beyond its scheduled six and a half minutes with the producers and directors cutting or dropping other segments on the fly to fit it in. Ron and Don, as they came to be known, also came to pop up throughout the evening, pre- and post-game.

Part of this was their immense popularity but it was also because both of them came to be the most powerful people on *Hockey Night*. Not even the producers dared cross them. The topics Cherry wanted to discuss were off-limits to other panelists and commentators. As long as this rule was observed no one had much trouble with Cherry, although some of the other broadcasters would chafe from time to time about not being able to discuss the same issue as Cherry.

But MacLean was involved with every aspect of the show. He came to be seen by his colleagues as the power behind the throne, the benevolent dictator whose "suggestions" became law. This was resented by some, although for the panelists on the show the biggest annoyance was MacLean's notorious habit of going over the list of supposed discussion topics before the show and then throwing stuff from left field at them when the show started.

MacLean always grew exasperated when I would bring up his reputation as the real boss of *Hockey Night*. He insisted he was only trying to make the show better, not run the place.

"Honestly, that's not true," MacLean said on one occasion. "You must know the league had a great say [in the CBC days] and always will have. Obviously, sitting with Grapes [Cherry], he and I discuss ideas so I have a little bit of a hand in a pretty important element of the show. But I always say at the end of the day it's a six-and-a-half-minute element out of a six-and-a-half-hour broadcast. To paint me as a power broker, I've always thought that was [inaccurate]."

MacLean also protested there were many executives above him at the CBC who had way more say in the program than he did. As for his colleagues, he said the most he would do is say, " 'What do you want to do tonight and I'll help you get there.' That was as involved as I was other than I was certainly on the front edge of getting music to be a big part of the opening to the telecasts."

The use of the musical montages, another CBC tradition, began to decrease in the first season of the Rogers version of the show and the first public controversy erupted around the amount of time allotted to *Coach's Corner*. Under Scott Moore and Gord Cutler, it was determined MacLean and Cherry would get five minutes in the first-period intermission and no more. This was to allow time for other features developed by Rogers for the time period. But it also had an important symbolic function: to show the entire staff that with the Rogers regime it was the producers who were in charge, not MacLean and Cherry.

MacLean was no longer in a good position to challenge authority and wisely decided this was not a battle to choose. So he made sure Cherry stuck to the script and did not allow him to keep talking. By November 8, 2014, Cherry was fed up. It was clear from the start of that night's show he was going to force the issue. He led off with, "I have to hurry. I only got five minutes, eh? This is what they call phasing a guy out. Y'know what I mean?"

In the main, MacLean resisted any temptation to openly join the pushback. But he did slide in a subtle rejoinder when he responded to the phasing-out crack: "At least you are still in the phasing process," to which Cherry replied, "Yeah, yeah, you're phased out."

There were six references by Cherry to the time limit during the five-minute segment. He threw up his arms in frustration at one point. "I don't have much time, as usual, folks," was an early shot, followed by "We over yet?" and then "I gotta talk fast, boy. You gotta pay attention to me, because I don't get much time." The segment ended with Cherry glaring off-camera.

Cherry's stand got the reaction he knew it would. At least from the media and the public. There were lots of stories in the newspapers and online in the next few days as well as discussion on radio shows. But it was obvious Cherry was not able to bull-doze management into more time. He was not disciplined for his show of temper but he did not get Cutler and Moore to budge on extending his time. Cherry even sounded contrite in his interviews the following week.

"Sometimes I have a little too much coffee, I guess," was his favourite line to questioners. He told *The Globe and Mail*, "We got it straightened out," but did not want to discuss the matter any further: "I'd just as soon leave it if you don't mind."

As the former head of CBC Sports, Moore was an old hand at wrangling Cherry, either with the man himself or with senior management. He was also well aware the *Hockey Night* staff was watching carefully to see if the new regime would stand its ground with a star known for tantrums.

"This is the first mildly controversial thing he's said [under Rogers]," Moore said, adding it was a "tempest in a tea pot."

All the media calls about Cherry, Moore said, were "good news, because it means people are watching the show." ·

The interesting response came from Cutler. "We're happy to have *Coach's Corner* as part of our show. It's a great asset but it's one of the assets we have every Saturday night," he said. Cutler referred further enquiries to Moore but his meaning was clear— *Coach's Corner* was no longer teacher's pet.

As the season progressed, that became clear to the viewers as well. MacLean and Cherry did not pop up before or after the games anymore. They had their five minutes after the first period and that was it.

The viewers, though, seemed to think the time allotted to Cherry by Rogers was just about right. Six weeks into the 2014–15 season, the Angus Reid Institute released an online poll of 1,504 Canadian adults. They were asked what they thought about the new show and its personalities. When it came to Cherry, 38 per cent of those polled said his time on the show is "the right amount." Another 26 per cent said Cherry's time was too much, which means only 36 per cent of the viewers thought Cherry's time was "too little."

The big question, of course, was what the poll respondents thought of George Stroumboulopoulos as MacLean's replacement. The answer, which in hindsight could have been taken as a harbinger of what was to come, was not much. When asked if Stroumboulopoulos was a credible replacement for MacLean, 60 per cent of the respondents said no with an almost even split between men and women. And 74 per cent of them felt MacLean's reduced role on *Hockey Night* hurt the brand.

On the question of which version of *Hockey Night* they preferred, there was more ambiguity. The CBC show was favoured by 45 per cent and only 14 per cent liked the Rogers version more. However, 41 per cent said they did not have a preference.

The early ratings of the new show also reflected ambivalence on the part of the audience. Rogers did not charge out of the gate as it hoped but neither did the broadcasts fall flat. Over the first eight weeks of the 2014–15 season, the average weekly audience for the first game Saturday night was up slightly from the same period the year before and down significantly for the second game. The Wednesday audiences were up from 2013 but the numbers for Rogers' *Hometown Hockey* on Sundays were troubling.

The *Hockey Night* early games, which generally featured the Maple Leafs and other Eastern Conference teams, drew an average of 2.2 million viewers through November 22, 2014. That was a 1-per-cent increase from the same period in 2013. The second, or Western Conference game, drew 860,000, a drop of 17 per cent from one million the year before.

Rogers executives were pleased with the Wednesday results, which showed an average audience of 974,000 through November, an increase of 230,000 on TSN's midweek games, which were not all shown on Wednesday night. The increase was fuelled by the Leafs' season opener against the Montreal Canadiens, which drew 2,025,000 viewers to Sportsnet. That was a record audience for the network but it was down 13 per cent from the Leafs' 2013 opener, also against the Habs, carried by the CBC, which had a greater reach than Sportsnet.

Ron MacLean, Tara Slone and *Hometown Hockey* were not an immediate hit. Through November 21, the broadcasts drew an average audience of 664,000 on City. That ranked the show 18th among the top 20 Canadian shows, well behind the CFL playoffs on TSN (1.2 million). Scott Moore countered that *Hometown Hockey*'s audiences were better than the entertainment programming carried on City the previous year.

There was also some aggravation with Bell Media as the first season under Rogers started. Bell was not happy the GamePlus mobile app was only available to Rogers' customers. When paired with the GameCentre Live streaming service, the GamePlus app allowed the viewer to choose extra camera angles and run replays. Bell filed a complaint with the CRTC that by restricting the app to its own customers, Rogers was hurting GameCentre Live customers who bought the service from another provider but could not get GamePlus because they were not Rogers customers. Rogers argued it was the one that invested in and developed the app. Its defence to the CRTC argued the app was covered by an exemption for digital media.

Guy Laurence, the combative British telecom executive who replaced Nadir Mohamed as Rogers' CEO, created some headlines with a direct shot at Bell. "With respect to crybaby Bell, what can I say?" Laurence said to reporters and analysts in late October on an earnings call.

This was an important fight for Rogers because there are three ways for the company to pull in revenue in hopes of making a profit by the end of the 12-year NHL rights deal. French-language television is technically the fourth revenue generator since TVA Sports pays Rogers $65 million annually for the national rights and the NHL essentially gives Rogers a $60-million annual credit for forcing RDS to pay that much, but those numbers are mostly fixed for the duration of the NHL contract. On the other hand, Rogers can increase the revenue from advertising, digital and mobile subscriptions and cable subscriptions.

The most important in that group are the digital and mobile subscriptions, which is why the GamePlus app is so important. It is tied to the NHL streaming services, so anything that might give Rogers a leg up on Bell and the other cable and wireless companies in selling those services is big. The advertising market is difficult to control unless ratings take off because advertisers keep a tight grip on their budgets. The continuing slide on the cable side of things makes it the worst of the three to raise money. On the same call Laurence made to take shots at Bell, he had to announce a 1-per-cent drop in cable revenue for the quarter because of subscriber cancellations. But Rogers still turned a profit of $1.3 billion in the quarter that ended September 30.

In mid-March 2015, the CRTC finally made a ruling on the GamePlus app. It went in Rogers' favour. The commission decided as long as the app "is not created mainly for traditional television" it could be exclusively used by Rogers since the company developed the product. Bell argued the app was linked to conventional television programming but the CRTC decided it was intended for digital viewing. The CRTC also encouraged companies like Bell to develop their own digital services that would be valuable to their customers.

As far as the broadcasts went, the early reviews were mixed but on the positive side. The chief complaint for the glitziest show, *Hockey Night in Canada*, was that Rogers was so determined to present an updated version of the show it was too busy. There were far more segments than in the CBC version, with analysts showing off the puck wall and its fancy statistics, getting out hockey sticks to demonstrate a play on the floor-rink and then moving over to panel discussions. Stroumboulopoulos literally walked through it all, strolling around the set to introduce segments, although he did sit down in the armchair section for interviews. This is where Stroumboulopoulos was at his best, interviewing various hockey types. His lack of hockey knowledge—Stroumboulopoulos was more of an enthusiastic fan than authority of the game—was not a problem because his interviewing skills made that irrelevant.

"We live in a very ADD society and the pace, well, we felt it needed to change," Moore told the *Toronto Star*. "If you look at our peer group in the US, it's fairly similar, with lots of shorter segments."

Two new stars were born in the early months. The first was former NHL player Nick Kypreos, who became popular on Sportsnet a few years earlier by working much harder than your average retired jock and combining that with his colourful personality. Kypreos was a fighter when he played and he brought that feistiness to television, never hesitating to engage his colleagues in a verbal skirmish. He mixed well on the panels with CBC holdover Kelly Hrudey and quickly became known to a new set of viewers for his strong opinions. The second was Elliotte Friedman, who was actually a CBC veteran of the show. But he was given a higher profile on the new show and would pop up on the panels as well as a news-and-comment segment with Damien Cox and do some features. While Friedman could crack the odd joke, his mostly earnest manner and ability to explain even complicated matters quickly and simply established him as the leading news-breaker on the show and his star rose as the season went on.

Unfortunately for Rogers, the first eight weeks of the season was the best period for the ratings. Sparked by an unexpected slide out of the playoffs by the Maple Leafs starting in January 2015 and the continuing drain of viewers for any kind of television, there was a 16-per-cent decline in Saturday-night audiences over the entire season compared to 2013–14's average audience of two million.

Rogers also did not fare well in the NHL's special events, as just 1.5 million people watched the all-star game, a drop of almost one million from the previous game in 2012 (the 2013 game was a casualty of the lockout). The annual outdoor game on January 1, 2015, this time between the Chicago Blackhawks and the Capitals at Nationals Park in Washington, DC, drew just one million viewers, down almost 2.6 million from the 2014 game. However, that was understandable since the 2014 game featured the Maple Leafs versus the Detroit Red Wings and fans were likely getting weary of the outdoor games after the NHL started putting more of them on the schedule.

The playoffs were a different story. Five Canadian teams advanced to the post-season, which promised a ratings payoff even though the Maple Leafs were not among them. Rogers had the bad luck that four of the Canadian teams played each other in the first round, which guaranteed only three teams at the most would advance. Still, Rogers drew an average of 2.4 million viewers for the games featuring those five teams: the Montreal Canadiens, Vancouver Canucks, Calgary Flames, Winnipeg Jets and Ottawa Senators. Overall, first-round audiences were up 36 per cent over the first round in 2014.

With only the Canadiens and Flames advancing to the second round and with both teams going no further, the Rogers ratings party ended there. The Stanley Cup final was a bigger hit on US television than in Canada, thanks to the big-market Chicago Blackhawks beating the Tampa Bay Lightning in six games. Audiences in Canada averaged 2.4 million for the six games of the final, which was a 12-per-cent decline from the 2014 final between the New York Rangers and Los Angeles Kings. Over the entire playoffs, the CBC and Sportsnet had an average audience of 1.5 million. That was a 2-per-cent drop from 2014 when an average of 1.53 million viewers tuned in on CBC and TSN.

But Rogers company executives declared the year a success. In the one year between June 2014 and June 2015, Sportsnet beat TSN's monthly average audience in the majority of months for the first time, drawing an average of 167,000 viewers per month, 9,000 more than TSN. Bell Media executives fired back that Rogers was cherry-picking its one-year period because it just happened to exclude TSN's last run with the NHL playoffs in the spring of 2014 and include Sportsnet's first playoff run in the spring of 2015.

Guy Laurence went one step further, claiming Rogers made a 10-per-cent profit on the NHL rights deal in the first year. "And, given it's our first year and we've learned a lot and all the rest of it, I don't see why it won't be profitable ongoing," the Rogers CEO told *The Globe and Mail*. There was a lot of skepticism in the broadcast industry about that claim, although the structure of the rights payments made a profit possible.

Gary Bettman wants more than almost anything to show the NHL owners that league revenues are steadily rising. The $5.2-billion deal worked out to an average of $433 million a year but it was not paid out that way. The first year saw Rogers pay the NHL the lowest amount with the payments rising steadily for the rest of the 12 years.

But just what Rogers paid the NHL in the first year has never been confirmed by anyone in position to know. There was, according to a broadcast source, a lump-sum payment of $150 million to the league in the summer of 2014. This was supposedly separate from the first annual payment, which—according to several media reports—was $300 million. But with the TVA Sports payment of $65 million and the NHL considering RDS's regional rights payment of $60 million as coming from Rogers, that eased much payment pain. Those media reports also said the payments rose in increments over 12 years to $500 million in the final years of the deal. This jibes with something Laurence told *The Globe and Mail*, that the annual payment rose by a single-digit percentage amount every year.

But given the dollar amounts in question, that would mean a jump in payments to the NHL of $20 million every year. Squeezing more advertising revenue and more subscription revenue out of advertisers and customers to cover that annual $20-million increase would be a never-ending challenge, especially if the ratings did not rise as well.

Rogers was not the only one having a rocky ride with the deal. So was the NHL, thanks to the Canadian dollar. When the deal was announced on November 26, 2013, the Canadian dollar was worth 94 cents US. By late March 2015 the Canadian dollar was down to 78.2 cents before getting back to the 81–82-cent range in April, where it stayed over the next two years, through the fall of 2017.

For reasons never explained by Bettman, the Rogers contract is paid in Canadian dollars. This doesn't make any difference to

Rogers, but it was a rare misstep by Bettman, as the NHL generally operates in US dollars. Thanks to the dip in the Canadian dollar, according to an NHL governor, the league took a 17-per-cent haircut in the first year of the deal, based on where the dollar was when the deal was signed. If the league did collect a total of $450 million (Canadian) in the first year of the deal, then $76.5 million was lost to the currency dip.

The biggest surprise of the first year of the contract with the NHL had nothing to do with television ratings or advertising revenue or cord-cutting. It was the sudden resignation of Keith Pelley as president of Rogers Media in April 2015. This came as a shock even to his good friends, as Pelley confided in very few people that he was leaving to become the chief executive officer of golf's European Tour.

However, once they had some time to think about it, those who knew Pelley well were not surprised. The 51-year-old had a history of knowing when to move on in his career—or getting out when the getting was good, a few cynics said—and it was always to something better or, in the case of his couple of years running the Toronto Argonauts, something that matched his passions.

Running the European Tour, according to Pelley, was "a once-in-a-lifetime opportunity." He was a long-time golf nut and said, "I love golf and given I'll never be a professional golfer, this truly is the next-best thing." He walked away from a job that paid $1.8 million in salary and bonuses in his last year at Rogers, but Pelley probably signed up for something better in the pay packet, as the European Tour is second only to the PGA Tour in prize money and prestige. Plus the job included a house on the famous Wentworth Club in London and a high profile in Europe.

Observers noted Guy Laurence cleaned house when he took over as Rogers' CEO in December 2013. Fifteen months later, when Pelley quit, that made it at least seven departures in the senior executive ranks at the company. But those close to Pelley said he left by choice.

Certainly Pelley received a nice send-off from Laurence, who said in a statement, "Keith has done a tremendous job for the company over the last five years and I'm delighted for him and his family."

Nevertheless, of the three men most responsible for bringing the NHL rights to Rogers—Pelley, Nadir Mohamed and Scott Moore—only Moore remained one season into the deal. And rough waters were ahead because by this time the Maple Leafs' new president Brendan Shanahan would make it known the team was going to be stripped bare for the most radical rebuild in franchise history. "A lot of pain," was the favourite answer of MLSE and Leafs executives when asked what lay ahead for the fans. The same could be said of Rogers given what was in store for the television ratings.

10

THE FALL

E arly in the summer of 2015, Rogers announced veteran television executive Rick Brace would replace Pelley as president of Rogers Media. Brace was head of specialty channels and CTV production for Bell Media when he was hired by Rogers. However, he spent a lot of time as a sports producer and director with the CBC and TSN before taking over the latter network as president in 1998. During his years as TSN president, Brace developed a good working relationship with Bettman and that no doubt played a role in getting the Rogers job.

But insiders said Brace was also hired for his expertise in trimming budget fat, something he would need to do in his first year on the job. While Rogers Media announced a profit of $90 million in its most recent quarter at the same time as it noted Brace was Pelley's replacement, the previous quarter, from January through March 2015, saw an operating loss of $32 million. The loss was blamed on the higher expenses for hockey and lower than expected advertising revenue.

The trouble for Brace was there was no relief in sight on the hockey front. Thanks to a decision by Maple Leaf Sports and

Entertainment back in late January to approve a radical tear-down and rebuild of the franchise, the Maple Leafs were primed to be a bad hockey team for a long time. With the team once again turning into that Brian Burke 18-wheeler going off the cliff midway through the 2014–15 season, head coach Randy Carlyle was fired on January 5, 2015, and replaced by assistant coach Peter Horachek. The rest of the season was a death march, as the players barely put forward an effort and the Leafs finished 15th out of 16 teams in the Eastern Conference.

In April 2014, not long before he announced he would step down as president of MLSE, Tim Leiweke appointed Brendan Shanahan the president of the Maple Leafs. After retiring from his Hall-of-Fame playing career in the fall of 2009, Shanahan worked for the NHL in various capacities, most notably as director of player safety or league disciplinarian. The Leafs job was his first experience at running a team, so Shanahan let it be known he planned to spend the first year studying the organization and getting his feet wet.

It did not take a full year for Shanahan to move into action. At the end of January 2015 he met with the MLSE board of directors and convinced them to approve his scorched-earth plan. He decided the only solution was to tear the organization down to the ground and rebuild slowly. The board, which rejected such plans in the past from Leaf managers, gave its blessing.

Three months later, Shanahan started cleaning house. His broom swept from top to bottom as just about everyone from general manager Dave Nonis to the coaches to the scouts to the training staff to the media-relations people were fired. Shanahan then pulled off a coup by convincing Mike Babcock, long considered the best coach in the NHL who resigned from the Detroit Red Wings because he wanted a new challenge, to sign an eight-year contract. Then Shanahan's mentor when he was a young player with the New Jersey Devils, Lou Lamoriello, signed on as GM.

Despite the presence of two of the best ever at their jobs, Shanahan, Lamoriello and Babcock said this would be a long, slow rebuild, done properly by drafting and developing young talent. As noted earlier, "a lot of pain" was the catchphrase, especially when it referred to the coming season. The unstated goal was to finish last overall in the 2015–16 season in order to have the best chance in the NHL draft lottery to land teenage sensation Auston Matthews. While Connor McDavid, taken first overall in 2015 by the Edmonton Oilers, was hailed as Sidney Crosby's successor as the next great superstar, Matthews, who grew up in that great hockey factory of Scottsdale, Arizona, was considered a generational talent nearly the equal of McDavid.

Brace, Scott Moore and the rest of the Rogers executives were silently cheering hard for the "Shanaplan," as it was known, to bear fruit quickly. The second half of the 2014–15 season was an ugly one, ratings-wise. One source said by the end of the regular season the ratings for Leafs broadcasts fell 60 per cent from the two million viewers who watched the Leafs–Canadiens season opener. The smallest audience was the 121,000 that saw a game against the Columbus Blue Jackets on April 8, 2015, on Sportsnet, although the Leafs somehow drew 2.3 million viewers on CBC and Sportsnet for their regular-season finale against the Habs.

The scary part of the Leafs rebuild for Rogers was the length of time it might take. In a salary-cap league like the NHL, 10 years to remake a franchise was not out of the question. The Chicago Blackhawks took eight years from 2002 when they drafted Duncan Keith, the first of the nucleus of star players that would sustain them, to a Stanley Cup win. Eight years represented two-thirds of the Rogers contract. This prospect was mentioned to Keith Pelley shortly before he left Rogers. He smiled weakly and said, "We have our faith in Brendan Shanahan."

Moore was also hopeful of a faster Leafs rebuild. In the meantime, he anticipated the curiosity of Leafs fans about Babcock in his first season as head coach would perhaps cushion at least some of the ratings shock. Another potential solution was Connor McDavid. Sportsnet planned to show up to 32 Edmonton Oilers games nationally in 2015–16 to showcase the budding superstar in his first NHL season.

When it came to the hockey broadcasts, no major changes were made for the second season aside from cancelling the late-night edition of *Hockey Central*, the highlights show. While some Rogers insiders said it was part of the overall Rogers budget cuts, Moore said the reason for dropping the show was mostly due to a programming problem because it could not be fit into a consistent time slot as none of the games ended at the same time.

The biggest loss to *Hockey Night in Canada* came from behind the scenes. Sherali Najak, the long-time senior producer of the show, resigned his post in favour of a reduced role as a game director. He also volunteered to serve as a mentor to younger broadcasters. He was replaced by Mark Askin, another veteran producer who had earlier stints at *Hockey Night* under his belt before taking over the game broadcasts at Leafs TV.

Najak was considered the best game producer in Canada, skilled at juggling all the things going on at once in a broadcast. He never gave a detailed explanation of why he wanted a reduced role other than to say he "just felt I needed a change." A few people close to Najak said he was seeking a better work-life balance and was worried about how the budget cuts everyone knew were coming would allow the staff to maintain *Hockey Night*'s excellence.

The show's most popular duo, Don Cherry and Ron MacLean, wound up having a good season overall after a slow start and public tantrum by Cherry over the time allotted to *Coach's Corner*. MacLean embraced his role as the on-location host for *Hometown Hockey* and proved to be a good company man with his interaction with the communities that played host to the show. His willingness to hang out with the locals went over big with Guy Laurence and others in the senior management ranks of Rogers. They came to like the show as a way of building grassroots rapport with existing and potential customers and were not concerned with its disappointing ratings.

Hometown Hockey drew an average of 567,000 viewers in its first season on Sunday nights. That was a 19-per-cent increase from the non-sports programming City carried in the previous year but it was 7 per cent less than TSN's non-Wednesday week-night games in 2013–14. "The community and the stories were the stars," Moore said of the show.

Cherry declared the first season of the Rogers version of *Hockey Night* a success even if he still wasn't convinced *Coach's Corner* was best at five minutes. "It went great for me," Cherry told *The Globe and Mail*. "*Coach's Corner* is a little shorter than I wanted but everything worked out so I have no complaints at all."

If there was anyone who was still unsettled about his role with *Hockey Night* it was probably George Stroumboulopoulos. The sentiments of that Angus Reid poll early in the season, which found 60 per cent of the Canadians surveyed did not think Stroumboulopoulos was a credible replacement for MacLean, were repeated on social media. Stroumboulopoulos came in for more criticism on Twitter—the forum of choice for NHL fans in expressing their views and getting their hockey news—than anyone else. Even the acerbic Glenn Healy, who was the most polarizing of the broadcasters, took less heat than Stroumboulopoulos.

Canadian hockey fans are an older and conservative lot who did not take to the 40-something host with the 20-something wardrobe. Middle-aged hipster shtick was not their style and they let loose in the comments sections of online media stories, Twitter and Facebook. Stroumboulopoulos never said anything publicly about the criticism but those close to him said it troubled him.

At this point, a lot of the anger could be put down to the reluctance of people, especially older people, to accept change and the unhappiness of the large numbers of Leafs fans with their team. Stroumboulopoulos clearly did not live and breathe hockey like MacLean, but his bosses thought he did a good job in his first year.

"My assessment of George is he did exactly what we asked him to do," Moore said. "We asked him to be more conversational, to be the everyman host as opposed to a host who was trying to compete with his analysts for hockey knowledge."

One off-season fix dealt with an issue that had echoes of former Bell Media executive Phil King's note that his company's bid for the NHL rights included the demand that it would have greater say over playoff start times than NBC, which was paying less money. In Rogers' first season, Bettman still allowed NBC to call the shots on the playoff schedule, which meant there were no prime-time playoff games on two Saturdays in May, much to the detriment of Canadian television ratings. Moore said this was the subject of much discussion and in the 2016 playoffs "I would be surprised to see afternoon games in the conference final."

As the second season approached in the fall of 2015, the tough times in broadcasting continued. There were job losses at Rogers, although the hockey department was shielded from the cuts. Things appeared worse at Bell Media, which was still profitable like Rogers but management at BCE demanded more cuts to maintain the profit margins.

Rogers got some relief from the surprise showing of the Toronto Blue Jays. Helped by a series of trades made by general manager Alex Anthopoulos that netted stars like Josh Donaldson, Troy Tulowitzki and David Price, the Blue Jays made a stirring run to the Major League Baseball playoffs for the first time in 22 years. This brought Rogers an unexpected bonanza at the box office, on television and online. The Blue Jays' attendance in 2015 jumped to 2.8 million, the highest in 20 years.

By the end of October, after the Jays' run ended in the American League Championship series, Sportsnet had an all-new top 10 of most-watched broadcasts in its history. All of them were Blue Jays playoff games, capped by the sixth and deciding game of the ALCS, which drew an audience of 5.1 million. The Jose Bautista bat-flip game that decided the division series was second at 4.9 million.

Now Sportsnet could not only claim to be number one over TSN in the battle of the Canadian sports networks, it was ahead of every other specialty network and was the number-two network overall in Canada in prime time. There was also a 450-per-cent increase in traffic on Sportsnet.ca in September over the same month in 2014.

The good news did not do much to boost the bottom line of a parent company that counts its annual revenue and profits in billions of dollars. For example, in Rogers' 2015 annual statement, its adjusted operating profit of $5 billion was the total of four company divisions—wireless, cable, business solutions and media. While Rogers Media, which owns the Blue Jays, Sportsnet, all the other Rogers networks, radio stations, publishing properties plus the company's share of MLSE, gets most of the media attention, it contributed the second-smallest share of operating revenue and profit to the bottom line, beating only the business solutions division.

Rogers Media's operating revenue in 2015 was $2.1 billion, up from $1.8 billion in 2014, and its adjusted operating profit was $172 million. Compared to the $3.2-billion profit posted by the wireless division on revenue of $7.7 billion, that was small beer indeed. While the $172-million profit was a $41-million increase over 2014, the problem was it was still down from 2012's $190-million profit thanks to ever-increasing operating expenses, which included all that money paid to the NHL.

In its annual report for 2015, Rogers said operating revenue at Rogers Media increased thanks to the Blue Jays, with increases attributed to the NHL deal and Sportsnet helping out. But print and television advertising revenue continued to decline as overall sports programming costs increased, led by the NHL deal.

The profits, despite the dips at Rogers Media, may sound like plenty to go around but the problem with a public company that trades its shares on the stock market is you are only as good as your latest quarter. The all-important goal is keeping the share price on the rise. As one of the telecom insiders put it, "After every quarter, no matter how well you did, when the next quarter starts you're back at zero." Combine that with the continuing slide in cable subscribers and advertising revenue and both Rogers and Bell maintained their ruthless cost-cutting.

Rogers Media announced in early 2015 it would cut 200 jobs and in November Bell Media said it was going to slash 380 jobs in Toronto and Montreal, with Toronto losing 270 of them. The Bell cuts included many high-profile media people and one long-running TSN program, *Off the Record*. Let go were hundreds of people from news anchors to reporters on radio and television to behind-the-scenes producers, editors, technicians and even receptionists.

The 2015–16 NHL season, the second under the Rogers banner, opened with a lot less optimism than the first one did. While the hockey staff was spared from the cuts going on in the rest of the company, they were well aware of the cutbacks. And the malaise set in with television audiences before the season was at the halfway mark.

Considering the Maple Leafs started the season every bit as bad as everyone was expecting, the ratings did not crater right away. And on the regional telecasts, some ratings took off. Unfortunately for Sportsnet, the biggest increase on the regional telecasts belonged to TSN, as the Ottawa Senators saw a 62-per-cent jump in viewers over the first two months of the season. This reflected an improvement in the team's performance and that pattern held for the other Canadian teams. The Edmonton Oilers, with Connor McDavid in the lineup, were up 19 per cent in their Sportsnet regional ratings through early December 2015 over the same period the year before. The Montreal Canadiens' regional English games, also on Sportsnet, had a more modest increase of 4 per cent. At the same time, the slumping Vancouver Canucks (27 per cent) and Calgary Flames (5 per cent) were both down regionally on Sportsnet.

On Rogers' national broadcasts, the *Hockey Night in Canada* ratings were down 7 per cent, which was not too bad considering those games mostly involved the Leafs. Regionally, the Leafs had a 9-per-cent decline on the games Sportsnet carried but dropped by 28 per cent on the TSN games.

However, that was as good as the ratings news got for Rogers. By late March 2016, audiences for the early game on Saturday's *Hockey Night in Canada* were down 16 per cent on average from 2014–15 to 1.66 million. In most cases those were Maple Leafs games. That marked the second consecutive 16-per-cent drop over the season from the two-million average the CBC reached in 2013–14.

There was no good news among the rest of the Canadian teams, either. None of the seven teams was headed for the playoffs, not even the Montreal Canadiens, who would miss the post-season for the first time since 1970.

The worst part of this was the damage done to the rosy projections Rogers gave advertisers in the summer of 2014, that audiences would increase by 20 per cent. With the numbers becoming even worse in the second season, broadcast insiders said the viewership for Rogers hockey broadcasts only reached 77 per cent of the forecast given to advertisers in the fall of 2015.

Broadcast sources said Rogers hoped to pull in $250 million in advertising revenue in its first season with the NHL deal. According to Barry Kiefl of Ottawa, president of Canadian Media Research Inc., that was an extremely ambitious target. Kiefl, who spent 18 years at the CBC and was the network's head of research, believed the CBC pulled in $175 million in hockey advertising in the last year of its NHL deal. He thought the best Rogers could do in its first year was a gain of a little more than 10 per cent to about $195 million. Just what Rogers managed in ad revenue is not known because it is not broken out separately in its financial statements.

When the ratings do not hit the targets set by broadcasters, advertisers are entitled to what are called "make-goods." This is free advertising time on future shows to make up for the smaller than expected audiences. Broadcasters build a certain number of make-goods into their budgets but when there is a tsunami of bad ratings like the 2015–16 NHL season, the make-goods take away a lot of advertising time that could have been sold to others, cutting even deeper into revenue.

The problem for Rogers was that the company was forced to give the make-goods in the 2016 playoffs. Usually, the playoffs are where the broadcasters really haul in the cash because those spots are not sold well in advance. If the ratings are good, which means a year lots of Canadian teams make the playoffs, then the rates are higher, the demand from buyers is higher and the money rolls in.

But on top of the bad news that none of the Canadian teams made the playoffs, the make-goods Rogers had to give advertisers ate up a significant chunk of the post-season inventory. So Rogers had to give out spots on its non-sports shows and even the highly rated Blue Jays games, which again reduced the advertising time the company could sell. Advertisers also started switching their hockey commercials to the Blue Jays as far back as the start of the 2015–16 NHL season, thanks to the baseball team's success. Some buyers had the right to do that but had to pay a premium for the switch because the Blue Jays' ratings were now much higher than hockey.

"It is kind of grim but unlike the fairy tales it is reality," said an advertising buyer who asked to remain anonymous to preserve a business relationship with Rogers.

Nevertheless, the combative Guy Laurence insisted the company would still turn a 10-per-cent profit on its hockey broadcasts for a second consecutive year. "It will absolutely, definitely, without any shadow of a doubt, make a profit, period," Laurence told reporters at Rogers' annual general meeting in April.

With all the unhappiness across Canada over the Canadian teams' collective mediocrity, led by the Maple Leafs' successful drive to finish dead last, it was no surprise the volume of complaints about Rogers' version of *Hockey Night* increased. By the time the 2016 playoffs started, social media fairly hummed with dissatisfaction.

The majority of the fans' complaints could be divided into two groups. The first and seemingly larger one said we hate George Stroumboulopoulos, bring back Ron MacLean. The second, which usually included members of the first group, hated the new, high-tech look of *Hockey Night*. This made a long-time staffer with the show laugh sarcastically. He said there were non-stop complaints about *Hockey Night* in the last few years the show was produced by the CBC. Viewers said Ron and Don were stodgy and out of touch, they didn't like MacLean's puns and complained the whole show was dated. "We were under siege," he said.

It was difficult to blame Rogers for this. The company conducted all kinds of research before the first season about what hockey fans wanted to see. The results went into the building of the state-of-the-art set, the segments on analytics and even having Stroumboulopoulos walk around instead of sit at a desk.

The way one veteran *Hockey Night* insider saw it, there were two problems. The biggest was that most viewers were in a foul mood because in every Canadian NHL city, the local team was awful. The other problem was too much change in the show all at once, which could be laid at the feet of Rogers executives.

"People just don't like change," the *Hockey Night* staffer said. "They will tell you they want change but they really don't."

Well, thanks to the ratings dive and falling revenue, with the non-stop complaints about the show also playing a role, viewers were about to see a world of change. Only this time it would be an about-face to the old version of *Hockey Night in Canada*.

This started with a bang even before the NHL playoffs were under way. Just before the regular season ended in April 2016, Gord Cutler, the head of production of all of the Rogers hockey broadcasts, was fired. This came shortly after the Rogers cuts touched the hockey department for the first time, when several staff members were laid off. Cutler was replaced by Rob Corte, who had been in charge of the Blue Jays broadcasts. Hockey was added to Corte's portfolio and he was named vice-president of Sportsnet and NHL production.

There was no comment from Moore about firing Cutler, with whom he had worked for years going back to Sportsnet's founding in 1998. All that came from Rogers management was a statement in a press release that was nothing but corporate-speak: "This change comes as part of our bigger company restructuring, which was announced at the end of January. While this has been a tough year with Canadian NHL teams out of playoff contention early, our commitment to the NHL has never been stronger. There is no correlation between today's change and our NHL deal."

Some Rogers sources said Cutler and Moore had their differences over game broadcasts but no one thought they were serious enough to warrant dismissal. The hint in the official statement that it was a financial move also prompted skepticism. While Cutler was certainly well paid there were lots of on-air people who were likely getting the same or better money than he was.

More than anything, it was the timing of the move that left most people in the industry scratching their heads. Firing the man in charge of the broadcasts on the eve of the playoffs, the busiest and most intense time of the season, was a strange one. More than a few of Cutler's peers wondered why Rogers could not have waited a couple of months and let him go when the rest of the changes would be made.

One person close to *Hockey Night* made some prescient observations in the wake of Cutler's firing. Harkening back to Cutler's firm hand in limiting the on-air time of Don Cherry and Ron MacLean, this person said, "it would be very interesting to see how much Ron is on during the playoffs. It would be interesting if he is on more." Cherry and MacLean in fact were on the air more in the absence of Cutler as the playoffs went on, which in retrospect was an omen of what was to come.

No one had any doubt by this time the Rogers cutbacks were going to be felt by the hockey people. The company originally said 200 jobs across Rogers Media were going to be lost, but as the ratings carnage continued in the NHL playoffs the cuts started even before the regular season was finished.

Back in March, with morale among Sportsnet's hockey people fading, their mood worsened when Scott Moore sent out a company-wide memo. He noted the problems with ratings and advertising revenue caused by the poor showing of the Canadian teams. Then he mentioned layoffs. Moore did not make a connection between the Canadian teams and layoffs but the employees sure did.

Hockey staffers said fewer freelance people were used towards the end of the season. This affected both on-air broadcasters like Billy Jaffe, who was often flown up from the US for games, and technical people. And once the dollar figure was reached for the annual in-kind fee for the CBC staff loaned to Rogers, they were no longer used because they had to be paid extra. If it was cheaper to use a local freelancer in a US city and save on the travel costs and extra pay for a CBC or even Canadian freelancer, then the local one was used. At least one Rogers insider complained this affected the broadcasts because the local freelancer in the US often lacked any hockey broadcast experience.

When the playoffs started, the decision was made to cut back to three Rogers game crews and use the fourth, with play-by-play man Dave Randorf, for spot duty. This saved production costs of $100,000 per game when the local us broadcast or NBC Sports production was aired instead.

The ratings for the 2016 playoffs were terrible from the start. Without a Canadian team in the mix, audiences were down 60 per cent in the first week from the previous year. No game drew as many as one million viewers, which was unheard of for the playoffs. By the end of the first round, the average audience on Sportsnet was 549,000, a 55-per-cent drop from 2015. The second-round audiences rebounded to 715,000 per game but that was a 52-per-cent decline from the previous year. The third-round audiences climbed again, to an average of 1.1 million, although that was down 11 per cent from 2015. The Stanley Cup final between the Pittsburgh Penguins and San Jose Sharks, drew double the average audiences from the conference finals at 2.2 million per game but that was 8.3 per cent less than the 2015 Cup final.

An indication of just how bad things were was that the live broadcast of the NHL's draft lottery on April 30 provided one of the best hockey audiences of the post-season on Sportsnet and CBC. Then again, with all seven Canadian teams out of the play-offs, fans of all seven of them had something to cheer for in the draw for the first overall pick. So, with Maple Leafs fans making up the bulk of the viewers, 1.57 million viewers tuned in, larger than any game audience to that point. The Leafs and their fans were rewarded for their tank job, as the Leafs won the right to draft Auston Matthews first overall in late June. Also cheering were Rogers executives, who knew the teenaged prodigy would speed up the Leafs' rebuilding efforts.

While Cutler's firing was a big surprise, at least to those in the broadcast industry, what was coming would set off shockwaves right through Canada's hockey fans. By this time, the looming job cuts dominated conversations among the employees. "There's tons of concern about that," one staffer said. "That's all anybody talks about."

Speculation about Stroumboulopoulos's future began among broadcast types in the final months of the season. Moving to the highest-profile sports broadcasting job in the country had not been easy for him. People friendly with Stroumboulopoulos said the constant criticism from social and regular media bothered him. One colleague pointed out Stroumboulopoulos spent most of his career in the entertainment field where "everybody kisses your ass." There is no face-to-face criticism in that industry, the colleague said, and then Stroumboulopoulos lands in sports where arrows are flying everywhere, from the traditional media, bloggers and social media, and he took most of it to heart.

There was also a strong belief that even though Stroumboulopoulos held one of the best on-air jobs in Canada, he regarded it as a transitional job. Several people who worked with him thought his ambition was to be a talk-show host in Los Angeles (where he maintained a residence) on a major US network. "He wants to be like Jimmy Fallon," one of them said.

However, the same people did not think Stroumboulopoulos was ready to quit his job. As it turned out, he did not get the choice. Sportsnet president Scott Moore, according to a source at Sportsnet, had been thinking for some time about making a change and restoring Ron MacLean to his old job. Sources said the first move was to make sure NHL commissioner Gary Bettman would not have a problem with the decision, given his relationship with MacLean. Several sources said either Rogers Media president Rick Brace or Moore went to New York during the 2016 playoffs to discuss the matter with Bettman. No objection was made, probably because Bettman appreciated the fact Rogers was hurting financially with the way ratings were going and needed to try something drastic.

Moore made his next move in mid-June when he asked MacLean to meet him at a small restaurant in the Long Branch neighbourhood in west Toronto. Moore told MacLean he wanted him to return as host of *Hockey Night*. MacLean was willing but only if he could also remain as host of *Hometown Hockey*, a job he genuinely came to love. This set off a series of negotiations because by doing both jobs MacLean could not be the host on the late Saturday game in order to travel to his Sunday assignment.

Before the negotiations were finished, news of MacLean's return was broken by *Toronto Star* columnist Dave Feschuk. It set off the predictable furor but it was clear from the reaction that most hockey fans were in favour of the move.

On June 27, 2016, Rogers dropped a figurative bomb on both its employees and the viewing public when the cuts were announced. It was confirmed Stroumboulopoulos was fired to make way for MacLean's return. David Amber, a reporter on the show, would be promoted to host the late Saturday game so MacLean could travel to the host community for *Hometown Hockey*. Then seven more firings were revealed among the Rogers hockey broadcasters.

Out as the between-the-benches analyst on the number-one *Hockey Night in Canada* crew was Glenn Healy, who still had at least three years left on his contract. He was the biggest surprise aside from Stroumboulopoulos, as broadcast insiders did not think Rogers would make a cut on its top broadcast crew. Also dumped from *Hockey Night* was commentator Damien Cox, although he was given a landing spot as Bob McCown's co-host on Sportsnet The Fan 590's popular supper-hour radio show, *Prime Time Sports*. Released outright were P.J. Stock, Billy Jaffe, Chantal Desjardins, Corey Hirsch and Leah Hextall, who all worked regional games for Sportsnet. The Saturday afternoon pre-game show on Sportsnet 360 was cancelled. Also let go were five producers, which brought the staff losses to 13 people. However, it was hard to put a proper

number on the total jobs lost because there were several job clas-
sifications on the broadcasts, from staffers to CBC people on loan
to freelancers and contract workers. Freelancers were dropped
and contracts were not renewed but it was not known how many
workers were affected.

One Rogers employee who survived the layoffs shook his head
as he thought about all of the optimism almost two years earlier
at the big staff party at the swank Toronto hotel. "We were at the
Ritz-Carlton, it was a crazy party and there was so much hope and
excitement. Half the people at that party are unemployed today.
It's just brutal," he said.

When it came to firing Stroumboulopoulos and what looked
like a pending return to the old style of *Hockey Night*, Moore
admitted there were probably too many changes at once.

"Two years ago, we made some changes to *Hockey Night in
Canada*," he said. "We were enthusiastic about the changes
but at the end of the day they did not resonate with hard-core
hockey fans."

The audience spoke, Moore said. "He worked extremely hard
but at the end of the day we are in the business of listening to our
fans. And as much as he appealed to some different demographics,
the hard-core hockey fan had trouble accepting that change."

Stroumboulopoulos did not make himself available for
comment then or later. People at *Hockey Night* who were friendly
with him said Stroumboulopoulos would say hello by text or email
over the summer but whenever anyone would suggest getting
together he would not respond. He has yet to return to a regular
spot on television, but Stroumboulopoulos remains active in
broadcasting with *The Strombo Show*, a Sunday-night radio show
featuring music and interviews that started in 2005 and moved
around various stations until it settled on CBC Radio 2 in 2009.

But Stroumboulopoulos, who had at least two years left on
his Rogers contract, did make his feelings known on Twitter in

a subtle way. On the day of the announcements he changed his Twitter profile picture to one of him and US broadcaster Keith Olbermann arm-in-arm. Olbermann spent the day on Twitter repeatedly blasting Moore for firing Stroumboulopoulos.

Funny thing, though. According to figures released by the CRTC, Sportsnet had a pre-tax profit in 2016 of $93.6 million, up nicely from $53.7 million in 2015. So there was still, despite the gloom, a rosy outlook on the bottom line at the end of the year.

EPILOGUE

The elephant in the room was addressed before the 2016–17 NHL season even started. Ron MacLean got his first interview with Gary Bettman out of the way during the World Cup of Hockey in September, which was carried by Sportsnet. It followed a meeting between MacLean, Scott Moore and Rob Corte, the new production chief.

"There was just kind of a gentle talk between Scott, Rob and me," MacLean told *The Globe and Mail*. "Let's, whatever we do, not throw this right over the cliff on the first interview." And he didn't. Bettman paused after answering the first question, said, "Welcome back," and the rest of the interview, about the NHL not playing in the 2018 Winter Olympics, went smoothly.

It may have been a different Ron MacLean as far as interviewing Bettman was concerned. But by the end of the World Cup it was clear the Ron MacLean back on their screens was the one viewers grew used to over the previous four decades. And once the NHL season started, most of the old version of *Hockey Night in Canada*, that familiar old sweater Canadians loved to wear, was back as well, even if the group was still on that fancy new set Rogers built.

Rogers pushed that notion hard leading up to the season: an old friend both figuratively in the show and literally in MacLean was back. A series of commercials featuring MacLean started running in September and they were as much a mea culpa from Rogers as an announcement the clock was turned back on the show. There was no sign of the fancy new studio, just a camera following MacLean through the newsroom as he talked about how Saturday night in Canada means hockey.

The response on social media was much warmer than anything *Hockey Night* saw in the previous two years. "I LOVE this Ron MacLean commercial. This is exactly what #HNIC was missing last two seasons," went one of the typical Twitter responses.

When the season opened, the glitzy high-tech effects were gone, along with the glass floors that doubled as hockey rinks. So was the puck wall and its fancy stats, as Rogers' research discovered analytics may be the newest craze in certain hockey circles but not among *Hockey Night in Canada* viewers. Ron was back behind the desk along with the discussion panels. Also back after a two-year absence was Scott Oake's interview show *After Hours*, which runs after the western game of the Saturday night doubleheader and is used to tell the players' stories.

"One of the pillars of our brand is innovation," Scott Moore told *The Globe and Mail*. "You want to be careful that innovation doesn't become change for change's sake. The viewers really feel they legitimately have an ownership stake in *Hockey Night*.

"You can literally change too much. I think in the excitement of the new contract we changed a fair bit. One of the things about Saturday night hockey is it's comfort food. It's something Canadians are really familiar with and the tradition goes back 63, 64 years."

Rogers also ensured Canadians could watch *Hockey Night* on the CBC for at least another eight years, until the end of the 2025–26 season. The original deal Keith Pelley pulled off with the CBC was for four years with Rogers having an option to renew for a fifth year. The option was quietly exercised in the spring of 2017, taking the contract through the 2018–19 season. Then Rogers Media president Rick Brace and Scott Moore negotiated a seven-year extension with the CBC.

The financial terms were not announced, although broadcast sources said the CBC would continue to provide the technical staff and the studio. That left unanswered the question of whether or not the CBC was able to squeeze any money out of Rogers for the use of its airwaves. However, the public broadcaster managed to improve the deal on one important front, as it secured the rights to stream all nationally broadcast games through the 2025–26 season. Those games will be seen on CBC.ca, the CBC Sports app and on a new CBC TV app the network launched in early 2018.

If everything that could go wrong did in the first two years, then just about everything that could go right did in the third season. As Pelley and Moore hoped back in 2015, the Maple Leafs' rebuilding program kicked into high gear faster than expected. With Auston Matthews leading the way with 40 goals in his rookie season, the Leafs climbed from 30th and last place overall to grab the eighth and last Eastern Conference playoff spot. Even better for Rogers, so did four other Canadian teams, the Montreal Canadiens, Ottawa Senators, Calgary Flames and Edmonton Oilers.

By the end of the regular season, the Saturday night games featuring the Maple Leafs and their exciting lineup of young players were routinely drawing audiences of two million, something that had not happened regularly in the first two years of the Rogers contract. The advertising inventory was sold out early in the season and for the first time there was no concern about make-goods.

The ratings did not go through the roof for the playoffs but on a percentage basis over 2016 they were impressive. There was a 94-per-cent increase in the average audience per game over the entire playoffs from 2016 to 1.61 million viewers. The Stanley Cup final between the Pittsburgh Penguins and the Nashville Predators drew 2.67 million viewers per game, a jump of 18 per cent from the previous year. The largest audience of the playoffs was Game 7 of the Eastern Conference final between the Penguins and the Senators, which drew 4.29 million viewers.

In the first round, the five series with Canadian teams drew an average audience of 1.8 million viewers on CBC and Sportsnet. That was triple the 549,000 average audience of the first round in 2016. The Leafs, of course, had the most-watched game in the first round when 3.64 million viewers saw Game 2 against the Washington Capitals.

By this time, Keith Pelley was immersed in his new job running the European Tour. But he said over the phone from London that he still took a lot of pleasure in the turnaround.

"It's been very gratifying because I certainly listened to some of the naysayers at the beginning," Pelley told *The Globe and Mail*. "But from what everybody tells me at Rogers, there's not many naysayers now."

However, Gord Cutler, the former boss of Rogers' hockey production, told *The Globe and Mail* it is time for broadcasters to realize television audiences are never going to go back to what they used to be. With the millennials often preferring to catch games by watching the highlights the next morning on YouTube rather than sitting through an entire broadcast on television, ratings standards need to be adjusted.

"One of the problems that the conventional broadcasters, whether it's Bell or Rogers, are having is they need to understand that there needs to be a new normal," Cutler said. "They're still struggling with comparing ratings for hockey to five years ago."

The *Sports Business Journal* commissioned a survey from 2000 to 2016 that discovered audiences for conventional television are aging faster than the general population. The median age for the NHL's games went from 42 in 2006 to 49 in 2016. Audience research done by Kaan Yigit, the president of Solutions Research Group Consultants Inc., of Toronto, aligns with Cutler's opinion when it comes to declining viewer numbers. His studies show audiences for the top prime-time television shows declined 11 per cent from 2016 to 2017, which makes the gains by Rogers in hockey impressive.

Despite the continuing shift of millennials and even older audiences to mobile and other online platforms, both Yigit and another Toronto consumer researcher, Charlton Insights president Gord Hendren, say two significant factors remain in Rogers' favour when it comes to making a profit by the end of the NHL contract. One is that conventional television is still the number-one platform and the second is that if the games are compelling and involve a team they are rooting for, the millennials will come to television.

Hendren first discovered this when he surveyed the television audiences for the Toronto Blue Jays when they made their surprise run to the 2015 American League Championship Series. A significant number of the three-million-plus audiences were young people, those aged 35 and under. It proved the adage in television now, that live programming remains impervious (for the most part) to the PVR and streaming generation.

Another of Hendren's surveys showed the interest and engagement of Canadian sports fans in the NHL increased in two of three age groups since 2016. There was moderate growth among 12-to-17-year-olds, a slight decline with millennials with the largest jump, 18 per cent, among those over 35. Hendren attributed this to the improved performances of the Canadian teams.

Best of all for Rogers, Hendren says, is his study shows "the Maple Leafs have a lot of up-side." From 2016 to 2017, the number of fans who called themselves a "big fan" of the Leafs increased 20 per cent to make up 24 per cent of those surveyed. The significance of this is since the Leafs reside in the largest market in Canada and only 24 per cent call themselves big fans there is much room for growth.

"We still think there are a lot of fans in the Toronto market waiting for the Leafs to prove themselves," Hendren said. "It's a large market with a long history of futility. The Leafs have given young fans a reason to be excited."

This is where Yigit is a little less optimistic than Hendren on the outlook of a profit for Rogers. His studies predict a rise in the number of Canadian households without a cable, satellite or other telecommunications package. In 2017, 22.1 per cent of Canada's 14.3 million households did not have one and Yigit expects that to hit five million by 2020, or more than one-third of Canadian homes.

With declining television viewers combined with increasing households that do not have conventional television packages, Yigit believes making money on the last two-thirds of the Rogers deal will remain a challenge. He says the bulk of the revenue Rogers earns on the NHL deal comes from the regular season and while millennials may come back to television for the playoffs they still prefer to watch game highlights on social media or other platforms during the regular season.

"If the game is boring, the kids aren't staying around for it," Yigit said. "I would agree [Rogers] probably will run to the finish line not having a disaster. But I'd say every year they have a challenge."

Executives in the broadcast industry agree but for different reasons. The bulk of the revenue from the deal still comes from television advertising, a couple of broadcast veterans with ties to Bell Media point out. The problem for Rogers is the payments to the NHL are structured so they rise every year for the entire 12 years. The sheer size of the contract, $5.2 billion, means Rogers faces an increase of something like $20 million every year. But advertisers do not have the budgets to increase their spending by a proportionate amount every year.

The other major revenue-producer is subscriptions. Rogers expected to sell more cable and wireless packages with a Sportsnet subscription to hockey fans. But thanks to the cord-cutters the decline in cable subscriptions is a drag on the increasing numbers of wireless, digital and streaming subscriptions. Sportsnet had 8.5 million subscribers in 2013 compared to nine million for TSN, which was the top sports network at the time. In 2016, both networks had lost subscribers, with TSN down to 8.5 million and Sportsnet down to 8.1 million. With the Leafs on the upswing, Sportsnet hopes its subscriptions will follow suit.

But in a broadcast world that is changing so quickly no one can predict what will happen next year let alone in the next decade, at least one executive sees the advantage lying with Sportsnet, although not even survival for either network is guaranteed. The key, said the executive, who has business relationships with both Rogers and Bell and wished to remain anonymous, is that Rogers owns the NHL rights for a long period of time and it owns the Blue Jays outright. So the company knows the programming costs for its two most important properties for the next decade, plus it owns all the platforms for those properties.

TSN, the executive said, does not have that luxury. Thanks to the recent arrival of giant corporations and other competitors as rights bidders in the sports broadcasting business, TSN will face continuous steep price increases for sports programming. Companies like Google and Amazon are buying up sports digital and streaming rights, the platforms that are growing quickly, and driving up the prices. They are wealthy enough to buy the rights in multiple countries. TSN already ran into the situation with its

Canadian NFL broadcast package. The network lost the Canadian digital and streaming rights in 2017 when the NFL sold them to DAZN (pronounced Da Zone), a British company that specializes in such deals.

While TSN, CTV and RDS carried weekly games, Bell and Rogers could no longer sell the NFL's all-access cable, satellite and streaming package, NFL Sunday Ticket. Starting in the fall of 2017, fans had to buy it from DAZN for $150 for the season and watch the games on an Internet-connected device like a smart TV, smart phone or tablet.

"TSN does the [Canadian] deal and at the 11th hour the NFL goes by the way, you don't have streaming rights," the broadcast executive said. "So TSN doesn't have *Monday Night Football* on TSN.ca anymore. That's gone, or on mobile or on anything. [Now] you can go see TSN games and any other game on DAZN. That's just the start.

"TSN, every single time a sports right comes up now for the rest of their lives, the digital giants are sitting there. They're already telling all the leagues next time your [rights are] up, we're up [to bid]. It's what happened in Hollywood. Netflix jacked the prices for everyone and hurt the CTVs of the world and the Globals."

The cable companies did get a small break when DAZN's streaming feed of the NFL games turned out to be of such poor quality there were waves of complaints from subscribers. By the sixth week of the NFL season, DAZN cut a deal with Rogers and a few smaller cable companies to carry the Sunday Ticket package again, although it was not back on Bell.

There is still no guarantee Rogers will finish well into the black by the time the NHL deal expires but their executives like their chances for a couple of reasons. One is the recent success of the Canadian teams appears to be sustainable, particularly in Toronto and Edmonton, even if the latter had a poor 2017–18 season. Both teams are well stocked with young talent led by two young superstars, the Oilers' Connor McDavid and the Leafs' Auston Matthews. Those in the executive suite at Rogers are already dreaming about a Toronto–Edmonton Stanley Cup final.

But the biggest reason for optimism, despite the punishing payments to the NHL, is that Rogers owns all the platforms, even the ones that have not been invented yet. And there are enough years left on the contract for the company to figure out how to monetize things like those social-media highlights the kids are watching.

"That's the magic," said former NHL marketing guru John Collins, who is now the CEO of On Location Experiences, which runs the hospitality side of big events like the Super Bowl. "Rogers has all those rights in Canada. If you're going to stick to a traditional broadcast model it will never work. But if you treat it like you are the gatekeeper for the most valuable content in the most hockey-mad, passionate country in the world and you're going to have it for 12 years on an exclusive basis, that's a pretty good deal."

Whenever Pelley is asked about the long-term prospects of the deal, he thinks of a conversation he had with Pierre Dion, who sold Québecor on the French-language sub-licence rights.

"Pierre Dion said it all along," Pelley said. "He said Keith, 'The first four years, people are going to say this is an okay deal. The next four, they're going to say it's a good deal and the last four, they'll say it's a great deal.'"

SOURCES

Publications that provided valuable background material include: *The Globe and Mail*, the *Toronto Star*, the *National Post*, the *Toronto Sun* and *Toronto Life*. Also helpful was *The Tower of Babble: Sins, Secrets and Successes Inside the CBC* by Richard Stursberg, an account of his years with the CBC (reprinted with permission from Douglas and McIntyre).

INDEX

Toronto Maple Leafs
  under Brian Burke, 11, 15, 31, 154
  CBC coverage and criticism, 6,
    10, 11, 12, 13–14, 16, 18–19, 47,
    56, 60, 71
  Leafs TV, 28, 175
  Ontario-born players, 11, 16–17
  owners, 74, 108
  ratings, 10, 28, 102, 103, 164,
    174, 179, 180, 185, 194, 196
  record, 63, 103, 153–54, 167, 173,
    179, 182, 193, 197, 199
  regional rights, 27–28, 35, 79,
    142, 143
  revenue, 29, 75
  second Ontario team, 127
  under Brendan Shanahan
    (rebuild), 171, 173, 174–75, 185,
    193
  See also Maple Leafs Sports and
    Entertainment (MLSE); *specific
    staff members and players*
trade deadline day, 142
TSN
  advertising, 143
  cutbacks and losses, 179,
  history of, 159
  monopoly, 112, 116–17
  morale, 141, 142
  NHL rights, 27–28, 38, 39,
    59–60, 81, 87–88, 97–98, 143
  Olympics rights, 29, 92–93
  other sports rights, 4–5, 37, 41,
    53, 144, 197–98
  personalities and staff, 36, 39,
    139, 140–42
  platforms, 35–37, 144
  ratings and audience, 36, 39,
    142–43, 164, 168, 176, 179, 180,
    197

revenue, 29, 144
subscriptions, 28–29, 60, 145,
  197
top sports network in Canada,
  38, 39
Tulowitzki, Troy, 177
Turner Sports, 59–60
TVA Sports
  competition with RDS, 73, 74,
    112, 114, 115–16
  revenue, 119–20
  Rogers partership, 82–83, 101,
    110–11,114, 115, 165, 169

USA Basketball, 56

van Gerbig, Barry, 122
van Riemsdyk, James, 154
Vancouver Canucks, 12, 14, 28, 31,
  79, 123, 154, 168, 180
Vegas Golden Knights, 125, 126
Videotron Centre, 120
Viola, Vincent, 128

Washington Capitals, 167, 194
Webber, Mike, 84, 90, 93
Weekes, Kevin, 135
Westhead, Rick, 36
Wilson, Ron, 10, 11, 15–16
Winnipeg Jets, 39, 79, 125, 126–27,
  143, 168
wireless contracts, pre- and post-
  paid, 24
world junior hockey
  championship, 39, 143

Yigit, Kaan, 195, 196

David Shoalts is a veteran sportswriter for *The Globe and Mail* who spent more than thirty years covering the NHL and the Toronto Maple Leafs. In 2009, he and Paul Waldie of *The Globe*'s Report On Business won the Outstanding Sportswriting Award from Sports Media Canada. He lives in Bolton, ON.